Slow Travel

reconnecting with the world
at your own pace

Penny Watson

Hardie Grant

TRAVEL

CONTENTS

ii

*Right: Conquering Mount Toubkal
in Morocco (see p. 181)*

INTRODUCTION

Travel has always offered a window of time, be it a weekend, a month or a year-long sabbatical, where we escape the routines and jadedness of the everyday. Getting away from it all on a beach holiday, a roadtrip or a city sojourn has acted as a restorative tonic, a time to reset, so that we can return to the daily grind refreshed and energised until the next holiday.

Now, more than ever, this need to reset – I mean truly reset – is part of the modern zeitgeist. Our connectedness to the digital world, as illuminating and groundbreaking as it is, also underscores a driving need for more downtime, more me-time, more time to connect to something other than our devices and our day-to-day responsibilities. This deep yearning can be seen in lifestyle trends such as wellness, mindfulness, holistic health, fitness, sustainability and even happiness. People are overhauling their diets, their routines and their lives to adopt and adapt to them. Entire magazines are devoted to these individual topics. Lifestyle pages are filled with self-help tips and feel-good stories, and bookshops are dedicating shelf space to these trends.

Slow travel is completely in sync with these impulses and desires. But what is it exactly? This growing movement embraces more immersive, curious, authentic and interactive travel experiences – it is travel to transform mind and body through connection with people and places. Slow travel is the antithesis of overcrowded tourist hot spots and tired checklist experiences; rather, it emerges from our longing to seek connection with ourselves and our lives in more intense and meaningful ways.

Its iterations are many and varied. In exploring slow travel, this book not only taps into the above lifestyle trends, it overlaps with travel trends including sustainable, nature-based, eco- and ethical tourism as well as what I call micro-travel trends such as cabins, tiny houses and pods. I also touch on emerging and niche trends including microadventures and forest bathing. Better me (*see* p. 48) has trip ideas for wellness and transformation; Cultural immersion (*see* p. 120) inspires travellers to get involved with the locals and upskill on the road; Unplugged (*see* p. 176) explores opportunities for digital detox and off-grid encounters. There are itineraries for long-distance train journeys, border-crossing boat adventures and roadtrips by bike and car through remarkable landscapes. There are chapters dedicated to sustainable travel, slow food and animal encounters. You'll discover incredible walks and epic hikes that will take you to mountain peaks, through jungles and across deserts under starlit skies. You will find islands, boltholes and remote escapes alongside ways and means of finding calm in big bustling cities.

While some itineraries are for those seeking self-discovery and a personal challenge in far-flung places, others are as easygoing and accessible as they are enriching. Perhaps most importantly, all of these slow travel experiences combine the opportunity for cultural understanding and insight with the serendipity and poignancy that only travel can ignite. I hope you find your slow.

Left: Banff National Park (see p. 69)

Overleaf: Three Glaciers Camp, Antarctica (see p. 75)

BEFORE YOU GO

Inspiration and ideas

So you've decided to go slow travelling. Here's the easy bit – inspiration and ideas. With pop-culture as your reference point, dive deep into books, movies, apps, playlists and more.

MUSIC

Tunes are obviously a very personal thang, so listen to your inner beat to make some compilations for the planning and the travelling. Perhaps some soothing backdrop music to dusting off the suitcase, an upbeat tempo to tracking down your hiking boots and a singalong soundtrack for your time on the road. Certain genres tap right into that slow travel mood – chill-out and singer-songwriters work for me (John's Legend's 'Ordinary People', 'Are you in' from Incubus, 'Lost in the Light' by Bahamas and Ziggy Albert's 'Stronger' for starters), but if 'ethereal wave' and 'uplifting trance' take you to that special slow place, go forth and bliss out.

MOVIES

There are plenty of essential movies that transport the willing mind to a faraway place in the press of a play button. If you're heading to France, *Amélie* and *Before Sunset* will make you fall in love with cobbled streets and cutesy cafes before you get there. *Hunt for the Wilderpeople* and *The Hobbit* are must-sees for travellers to New Zealand. *The Scent of Green Papaya* is a Vietnam classic and do yourself a favour and watch *The Sweet Hereafter* for a snippet of Canuck culture and place.

Delving a bit deeper, iconic films with slow journey themes about wilderness survival and self-discovery include *Tracks*, a true story about a woman's nine-month solo journey on camels across the Australian desert. *Wild*, starring Laura Dern and Reese Witherspoon, is a journey of self-discovery and healing along part of America's Pacific Crest Trail. Other survival films based on true stories and with epic scenery include *Into the Wild* about a young man's journey into the Alaskan wilderness and the mountain-climbing epic *Touching the Void*. There's nothing like a roadtrip movie to give you itchy feet and a dose of cabin fever. Start with classic counterculture movies such as *Easy Rider* about two hippies crossing America on Harley-Davidson choppers and *The Motorcycle Diaries*, a similarly evocative tale about Che Guevara and his friend Alberto Granado who ride from Argentina to Peru on motorcycles. Other uplifting roadtrip films include *Little Miss Sunshine*, *The Adventures of Priscilla Queen of the Desert* and *Y Tu Mama Tambien*. More travel flicks worth watching include *The Grand Budapest Hotel*, *Vicky Christina Barcelona*, *The Beach* and *Lost in Translation*.

APPS

There are as many meditation apps these days as there are monks (okay, not quite) including Smiling Mind and Headspace. But, for travellers, one in particular stands out. Calm, a mindfulness immersion app that hails from San Francisco, features ever-present Tamara Levitt's legendary 10-minute daily meditation sessions exploring themes such as renewal, self-compassion and closure as well as global ideas such as Hiraeth, a Welsh concept of longing for home, and the Japanese Ikigai, a reference to someone who lives in the present and doesn't let the small stuff get under their skin (which could be a useful tool while travelling). Calm's big point of difference is its sleep stories. Devised as a means of putting overactive minds to rest, they're also a catalogue of great slow travel tales that can inspire your next destination as much as send you off to the land of nod. Narrated with melodic voices and lyrically written, they can take you 'Meandering down the Oxford Canal', 'Stargazing on Stewart Island' in New Zealand or exploring Morocco's 'Hidden Forest' and 'The Birds of Yosemite' in the USA. Matthew McConaughey's dreamy story about the mysteries of the universe isn't a travel story per se but it's certainly inspiration for looking at the planet in a brand new way. The app also has sleep music – silk waves, summer breeze, star dance … the ideal accompaniment to long train trips, evenings under the stars or just alone time.

BOOKS

Even Kindle-addicted travellers should consider taking an emergency book or two. It's a guaranteed form of relaxation that doesn't rely on batteries or chargers. Reading a destination-themed novel is a great way to get a sense of the history, culture or political climate (or all three) of your destination and creates connections before you land. Some of my contemporary favourites include Michael Ondaatje's *Warlight* (England), Elena Ferrante's Neapolitan Novels (Italy), Martin Booth's *Gweilo* (Hong Kong), Xinran's *Sky Burial* (China and Tibet), Donna Tartt's *The Goldfinch* (New York and Amsterdam), anything by Tim Winton (Australia), Muriel Barbery's *The Elegance of the Hedgehog* (France), Orhan Pamuk's *My Name is Red* (Turkey), anything by Haruki Murakami (Japan) and William Finnegan's *Barbarian Days* (Hawaii and the South Pacific). You can't go past the classics either: Isak Dinesen's *Out of Africa* (Kenya), Graham Greene's *The Quiet American* (Vietnam) and Jack Kerouac's *On the Road* (USA) hail from vastly different eras but somehow capture a zeitgeist that still translates to now.

TIME

Though it would be lovely to travel without paying any attention whatsoever to time, realistically you'll probably need a clock so you don't miss that temple sunrise or departing tour/train/friend. But it doesn't have to be a clock on a screen. Dust off the smart-looking wristwatch that your grandma gave you years ago and slap it on your arm. Looking at your watch, rather than your phone, will help you avoid all those distracting alerts and messages that keep you from the job at hand – connecting with the world around you.

CAMERA

Similarly, to avoid the distractions of a digital device, consider swapping out your smart phone camera for a stand-alone camera. It could be a simple pocket-size handy cam, an SLR with all the lenses or even a retro 35mm camera. Certainly anything with film will make you think twice about taking endless photos of your tropical cocktails and will help develop skills and techniques so as to further scratch the surface of a destination.

JOURNALLING

'No-one has ever seen this place in the same way you're seeing it right now, right here, in this moment.' So says author Emma Clarke in her book *You Are Here: A Mindful Travel Journal*, which uses mindfulness techniques to promote a happy, peaceful mind while travelling. Even if you've never journalled or kept a diary, your slow journey might be the time to start jotting. On a practical level, keep notes and details of the places you visit, the people you meet and any changes to itineraries. Stuff ticket stubs and memorabilia into the pages. On a deeper level, take time to reflect on the feelings and sensations that each day inspires. Be meditative, embrace the best parts of your day and see where your flow takes you. If you're travelling device-free, or you're in a digital detox zone, a journal can fill the gap, rather romantically, where your smart phone used to be. They also travel well. Leaning against a tree or sitting on a mountain-top with your journal ensures you remain in the zone. What's more, when you get home you'll have an intimate and precious time capsule of your time away.

There are plenty of journals to choose from. The *Mindful Traveler: Exploration Journal* combines thoughts, prompts and reflections with space to set daily intentions.

The *Erin Condren PetitePlanner Travel Journal* has 28 daily spreads to log activities, meals, memories and spending (with illustrative and functional stickers to boot). For those who prefer to fill blank pages with scribbles and doodles, Compass Rose's leather-bound and stitched diary with an embossed compass on the front will remain a keepsake long after your travels are over; so too will the refillable *Maleden Spiral Bound Traveler Notebook* with retro British postmarks and stamps on its cover and a leather book-mark ribbon.

MAPS

If you know where you're travelling to (and even if you don't), get your hands on an old-fashioned hardcopy map. The bigger, the more crumpled, the more detailed, the better for pinpointing the stops on your journey as inspiration before you go, and as education while you're travelling. All too often we're left wondering what's beyond our screen-sized maps. Having a paper map gives you a zoomed-out version of the world on which you can draw arrows and scribble notes that say stuff like 'small gorgeous village where I met Tino' or 'best tacos ever here' or 'spent whole day doing yoga here'.

BODY

Slow travel can be as much about rebooting your body as your mind, be it through pampering, exercising, cleansing, energising or simply moving when you would otherwise be sitting at a desk or sprawled on the couch. To make the transition between your current day-to-day reality and the slow travel lifestyle, start making small changes to your activity levels, diet and routine in the months before you go. It doesn't have to be major: add an extra couple of hours of exercise a week to your routine or simply start walking an extra few blocks between home and work, and taking the stairs instead of the escalator or lift. Add something healthy to your diet – like a green fresh-pressed juice or some carrot and celery snacks – and take away one less-than-healthy pleasure, like that teaspoon of sugar in your tea or the extra chocolate biscuit. Explore some basic yoga stretches and poses – it's a travel-friendly activity that you can tap into anywhere, be it riding a horse through Mongolia or cruising down the Nile in Egypt.

CONNECTIONS

Slow travel is all about connections – connecting with each mindful footstep, connecting to the destination, connecting to nature and connecting with the people who join you somewhere along your journey. Whether these connections last a few minutes or a lifetime, all of them are important. There are small things you can do to instigate these connections. Learn five words in the language of the destination you are visiting, swap books with your fellow travellers, share your tips and secrets on places you have visited, shop locally, ask directions (rather than refer to your GPS) and buy one-off keepsakes from the people who actually make them. Taste different flavours and ingredients, explore new dishes, buy street food and talk to the people serving it. Choose public transport and cheaper travel options to get among the locals. Have random conversations. Simply connect.

MOSAICS

One way I like to get microscopic on the environment is to make small collages of the natural objects and artefacts I find along the way, be they feathers, shells, stones, bones or leaves. I've taken to doing this on beaches. My 'shell mosaics' are collections of remnant clam and mollusc shells, crab carapace, seaweed and eclectic marine flora and fauna washed up in the waves. They're beautiful when pieced together in the sand to create a colourful visual map that reflects the local marine environment and landscape. I particularly love creating shell mosaics on cold days when the waves look rough and foreboding, the wind whips around upturned collars and there's no motivation to don a swimsuit. But of course you can do it anytime, anywhere, with whatever you find – driftwood, smooth sea glass, the flotsam and jetsam of looking a little more closely at nature. Snap a pic to take home before returning your found objects to the landscape or watching them get washed away.

FOOTPRINT

Set out with the intention of leaving the smallest footprint possible by making your own plastic-free planet survival kit. In it, put a reusable bottle, keep cup (or a compact collapsible one as a space saver), stainless steel or bamboo straws, lightweight bamboo cutlery and chopsticks, hand sanitiser and a reusable shopping bag.

POSTCARDS

While you've got that pen out for journalling, why not scrawl a few words about your travels to a friend, your mum, an old boyfriend, your pet dog or you – the one you left back home when you took off to find a better version of yourself. Postcards are nice to receive but they're also fun to rediscover. Seeing your sepia-toned Italian beach missive pinned to your best mate's fridge a few months after you penned it is a recipe for a warm fuzzy post-travel moment. You could also consider writing thank-you postcards to anyone who deserves your gratitude on the road. You're more likely to write one if you write it straight away and what you write will be more heartfelt and of-the-moment than it will be if you wait until you get home. Travel karma at its best.

Overleaf: Coober Pedy is a pit stop on the Ghan, one of Australia's great train journeys (see p. 12)

MAKE TRACKS

Train journeys

Don't confuse a train commuting experience with a great rail journey. One has your face in offensive proximity to a stranger's armpit, the other is an escapist journey through some of the world's most jaw-dropping scenery. (But I see where you might get confused.)

There are many reasons why train travel fits nicely with slow travel. For starters, you have someone up the front driving and navigating – you're not getting lost, facing peak-hour traffic or trying to find a carpark. This leaves you with plenty of time to sit back, relax, eat, drink, read, journal and so on. But mostly it means you can look at the scenery. Each window frame is likely to be a new view, an ice-capped mountain as you come around a bend, a field of wildflowers, the striped greenery of wine country or a wave-washed beach. It's left to you to reflect, observe and take it all in.

... the ride was a slow-paced breather in the midst of a big travel adventure.

Many of today's great train journeys are a nostalgic nod to the hedonism of the 1920s with creature comforts and staff allowing you to really do nothing. But equally, cheap local trains are an opportunity to get an insider's angle on a destination. When my children were toddlers, my partner, Pip, and I had the impulsive idea of taking a family trip on Vietnam's Reunification Express train. The 1726-kilometre (1072-mile) journey along the east coast starts in northern Hanoi and ends 33-ish hours later in the southern Ho Chi Minh City. It travels at an average of 50 kilometres (31 miles) per hour, only slightly faster than in 1936 when it first journeyed along this path. We had done this trip previously as young backpackers and the repeat journey with kids was a different experience again, of course, but the ride was a slow-paced breather in the midst of a big travel adventure. The tropical heat blustering through open windows. Hamlets of flat-roofed houses clustered along the railway line. Locals waiting trackside on overloaded motorbikes for the boom gate to open. Hazy blue mountains, beaches, sparkling water, nets and boats filled window frame after window frame. The smell of noodles and overripe bananas. The waft of dried fish. The side-to-side motion of the carriages. Now, when I really want to put the brakes on routine and a hectic pace, a train journey is my default choice.

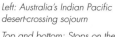

Left: Australia's Indian Pacific desert-crossing sojourn

Top and bottom: Stops on the Trans-Siberian Railway adventure

There's a certain romance that comes with train travel, especially when the rhythmic measured beat of a steam engine pulls you along the track. The symphony of a chuf-chuffing engine, the clackety-clack of tracks and the muffled toot-toot on a crossing approach has the mesmeric effect of taking you back to a time when the pace of life was just, well, slower. It doesn't have to be an overnight adventure, as long as the pace is right. At Victoria Falls you can hear the old 1920s steam trains coming along the track towards the iconic Victoria Falls Bridge before you see them. This engineering feat bridged the chasm between Zimbabwe and Zambia. The Royal Livingstone Express, in Zambia, leaves from Bushtracks Station in Livingstone and transports guests to the Palm Grove siding. The Bushtracks Express pulls out from the Victoria Falls Station and journeys to the Jafuta conservancy siding in Zimbabwe. During the three-hour round-trips, both luxury steam trains cross the iconic bridge showing off forget-me-not views of Victoria Falls and the wild beauty of the cavernous gorge from which the Zambezi River sends up clouds of mist – the trains, as they pass, catch the spray of the falls. The trimmings: waistcoated staff and a silver-service dining carriage add to the nostalgia and sure outdo a safari vehicle for comfort and calm.

BUSHTRACKS EXPRESS AND ROYAL LIVINGSTONE EXPRESS, ZIMBABWE AND ZAMBIA

....

-O- bushtracksafrica.com/steam-safaris

GLACIER EXPRESS, SWITZERLAND

In 1930, when worldwide railways were already operating modern electric locomotives, Switzerland's Glacier Express was still a steam-operated train – it earned a reputation for being the world's slowest express train (it wasn't a compliment). In the early 1940s the route converted to electricity, reducing travel time from 11 to eight hours. In today's fast-paced world, that's still slow, which is why we love it. The Glacier Express takes a snow-capped, ice-laden scenic journey across the magnificent Swiss Alps. The eight-hour trip between the ski resorts of St Moritz and Zermatt extends for 291 kilometres (181 miles) across mountainous terrain, deep ravines and rugged rockfaces; and through 91 tunnels and over 291 bridges – engineering marvels no less. Through the train's roof-high panoramic windows, you'll glimpse the Bies Glacier at 2000 metres (6500 feet), the only glacier still visible from the train, and the traditional timbered dwellings of Goms, a popular hiking region, sitting amid 3000-metre (9800-foot) peaks. The otherworldly Matterhorn comes in and out of view, and you'll pass the 2,033-metre (6670-foot) Oberalp Pass, the highest point of the journey. Also keep an eye out for the Grand Canyon of Switzerland – the 400-metre-deep (1300-foot-deep) Rhine Gorge; and the countless peak-top castles and fortresses of the Domleschg region. Food and beverages are delivered direct to your seat or you can check out the train's new Excellence Class for a seat at the Glacier Bar.

-O- myswitzerland.com/en-au/getting-around/glacier-express-st-moritz-zermatt.html

TRANS-SIBERIAN RAILWAY, RUSSIA

As epically long train rides go, the Trans-Siberian is the ultimate long-distance go-to. The rite-of-passage journey for adventurous travellers is often referred to as the Trans-Siberian Express, but the Trans-Siberian Railway is actually a network of railways connecting Russia's Moscow and St Petersburg in the west and Vladivostok (Russia) and Beijing (China) in the east depending on which route you take. The 9289-kilometre (5772-mile) route between Moscow and Vladivostok is the longest railway line in the world, passing through the heartland of Siberia and the vast grassy steppe of Mongolia, not to mention eight time zones. The direct route takes eight days, but that kind of speed is for cargo and locals. Tourists can really put their feet up and take weeks exploring the route. Intrepid's 20-day Trans-Mongolian Experience traverses three nations: Russia, Mongolia and China. Highlights include a stopover at magnificent Lake Baikal in a Siberian village, a stay in a ger camp in the Mongolian wilderness and experiencing a traditional Russian banya (a refreshing steam, wash, and birch branch 'massage') and pastry-making with a Russian family. Downtime on the train includes three overnight legs and, the longest, a three-day, four-night passage (90 hours) from Moscow to Irkutsk. Stepping from the train into the excitable cities of St Petersburg and Beijing at each end might prove overwhelming so be prepared for the change of pace.

-O- intrepidtravel.com/au/russia/trans-mongolian-experience-117623

THE GHAN AND INDIAN PACIFIC, AUSTRALIA

Norway has been playing around with slow TV for a decade, but Australia is just catching on to a trend that has been described amusingly as both boring and profound. Taking the country by quiet storm in 2018, progressive Australian broadcaster SBS hitched a GoPro onto the iconic Ghan train and streamed the epic 2979-kilometre (1851-mile) journey from Darwin in the north to Adelaide in the south. The nexus of travel and technology captured the attention and accolades of the online audience prompting SBS to produce a slow TV version of that other great cross-country train trip, the Indian Pacific, which runs 4352 kilometres (2704 miles) from Perth (on the Indian Ocean) in the west to Sydney (on the Pacific Ocean) in the east. While the slow television is hypnotic, the reality goes beyond expectation. The four-day Ghan trip takes 54 long, straight (mostly), mesmeric hours with the pace quickening only when the train stops at the tropical outback town of Katherine in the Top End, the Central Australian town Alice Springs (1500 kilometres (932 miles) from the nearest capital city) and South Australia's Coober Pedy, an eccentric mining town whose inhabitants live in caves to escape the desert heat. The Indian Pacific is already ticked off my bucket list. Its three-night, four-day journey takes 65 hours with stops in the quirky outback mining town of Broken Hill and, in stark contrast, Adelaide, famed for its surrounding wine regions. But it's the red-desert-dirt blur of the train crossing the Nullarbor Plain that I most remember. It is out there.

....

-O- *journeybeyondrail.com.au*

BELMOND ANDEAN EXPLORER, PERU

Complete with all the bells and whistles, this is South America's first luxury sleeper train and one of the highest train routes in the world. The one- and two-night getaways run between Cuzco, the ancient capital of the Incan empire, and the beautiful city of Arequipa with its Spanish-colonial heritage. In between, passengers take in the craggy mountain-tops and grasslands of the timeless Andean plains, and stop en route in Puno to see the constructed reed islands of Lake Titicaca. The 16-carriage train's exterior has blue-and-white hand-painted livery with a Peruvian textile motif. Similarly, the interior sidesteps the classic vintage train look by using earthy tones, textured leather and bright alpaca-wool throw cushions and art work – a nod to modern train travel. The service is all champagne and floral bouquets on arrival, heavy wool blankets on the beds, slippers and dressing gowns for lazing around in, and oxygen tanks and masks for guests on an altitude high. The journey basically ticks off Peru's big three in the most comfortable and contemplative way possible.

-O- belmond.com/trains/south-america/peru/
belmond-andean-explorer

THE BLUE TRAIN, SOUTH AFRICA

Luxury train adventures are often a throwback to the decadent years of the early 20th century when industry, commerce and society were on the move. Africa's original Blue Train, an opulent steam train that in its heyday boasted 'everything from card tables to ceiling fans, to hot and cold water on tap', was reinvented in 1997 with a new electric and diesel train traversing the old lines of tempered steel across the vast African sub-continent. The 39-hour, two-night journey between Cape Town and Pretoria is a 1600-kilometre (994-mile) scenic expedition through farmlands, rugged mountains, semi-arid desert, dams pink with flamingos, gold- and diamond-mining landscapes and the lush Cape Winelands. Off-train expeditions include the Kimberley Diamond Mine Museum (if the largest human-made hole on the planet is of interest) and an excursion to Matjiesfontein, a national museum made up of an entire village that has retained its Victorian-era history. Depending on where you start the journey, the behemoth beauty of Table Mountain begins or ends the adventure. The train exterior might not have the classic panache of the old engines (aside from the blue livery), but the interiors retain the wood-panelled elegance. Suites become comfortable lounges by day and ensuite bedrooms by night. Professional butlers attend to each carriage, and there's a dining car for fine wining and dining. Sit back and take it all in.

-O- bluetrain.co.za

COASTAL PACIFIC, NEW ZEALAND

When the devastating Kaikoura earthquake hit New Zealand in 2016, the iconic Coastal Pacific rail journey was put on hold. Two years after the tumultuous event, with restorations complete, the train was back on track and once again offers travellers a sensationally scenic seaside journey. The six-hour rail trip runs between Picton, in the Marlborough Sounds at the northern end of the South Island, and Christchurch on the eastern coast. Passengers can tilt the seat to enjoy views that take in 98 kilometres (61 miles) of rugged Pacific coastline, with the train passing within metres of the waves at some points along the track. You'll pass through Marlborough wine country and past iconic New Zealand vistas that combine brilliant green pastures and snow-capped mountain-tops – *Lord of the Rings* comes to mind. The train track passes through 22 tunnels and crosses 175 bridges including the Okarahia Viaduct, which arcs 21 metres (69 feet) above the beach below. It's definitely Insta-worthy. Stops include the whale-watching town of Kaikoura, dramatically placed between the base of the Kaikoura mountain range and the Pacific Ocean, and Blenheim wine country. Run by Great Journeys of New Zealand, the train departs from Christchurch each morning and returns from Picton each afternoon from December to April.

....

-O- greatjourneysofnz.co.nz/coastal-pacific

ROCKY MOUNTAINEER, CANADA

Getting up close and personal with the otherwise impenetrable Canadian Rockies is the main aim for anyone boarding the Rocky Mountaineer trains. At a leisurely speed of 45 kilometres (28 miles) per hour, the diesel-electric engines traverse four scenic routes across Western Canada, with stops including Vancouver, Whistler, Jasper, Lake Louise and Calgary depending on your itinerary. They're not overnighter trains (you can stay in hotels at stops along the way), but they're long distance with guests getting comfy in recliner seats and admiring the views thanks to glass-dome carriage-tops and wrap-around windows. I've taken the line from Winnipeg to Vancouver and it truly is a natural-world wonder. Once you've pulled the lever on that seat and settled in, it's like a Nat Geo movie rolling out before your eyes. You'll travel between glacier-capped peaks, over mountain passes and along rocky lakeshores that shine turquoise against deep green pine forests. Staff members are a wealth of information, pointing out potential bear snaps and the best view spots, serving food and drinks and more. The trips can be anything from two days (for travellers simply getting from A to B like I was), or up to 21 days with a cruise tacked onto the end. These latter lengthy journeys combine two different modes of slow travel in diverse natural environments, which can only be good.

....

-O- rockymountaineer.com

EASTERN AND ORIENTAL EXPRESS, THAILAND AND SINGAPORE

Cherrywood panelling, brass fittings and exquisite fabrics hint at the creature comforts on board the Eastern and Oriental Express. Passengers can also expect a turn-down service with slippers neatly placed under the bed. This is one of the world's most exclusive trains, a bucket-lister steeped in that fabled oriental hospitality. The two-night Bangkok–Singapore route takes in the lush tropical and rural landscape of Malaysia with a stop at Labu Kubong, a traditional village, and a side trip to the River Kwai, famed for its World War II Burma Railway history. Opt for a longer six-night journey to savour your time at stops including Cameron Highlands, a colonial-era tea plantation, and gorgeous Penang, with its multi-ethnic old town and decadent colonial architecture. On board, it's the slow route to heavenly relaxation. The dining car is a white-tablecloth affair with clinking glassware and low-lit table lamps. In the saloon car, choose a book from the reading room or indulge in a forty-minute foot massage. Just don't miss too much of that palm-studded rural scenery.

-O- belmond.com/trains/asia/eastern-and-oriental-express

On board, it's the slow route to heavenly relaxation.

Overleaf: The Eastern and Oriental Express journeys through South-East Asia

DESERT, WATER, ICE
Adventures in deserts, thermal waters and icy landscapes

Every weekday morning at about 6 o'clock, I feel the mattress moving as my partner gets out of bed. Soon after comes the sound of the shower, water raining on tiles. Then, like something worthy of Darth Vader, I hear his deep, measured, lung-filling inhales followed by slow exaggerated exhales. This daily cold-shower ritual is thanks to Dutchman Wim Hoff, an extreme athlete noted for his ability to withstand extreme cold. With world records for swimming under ice and completing a half-marathon barefoot on snow, he is worthy of his nickname Iceman. Hoff's theory dictates that ice-chilled water – be it cold-shower rituals or Arctic swims – has health benefits including rebooting the immune system and clarifying the mind. My partner has clearly been won over and, while the rest of us might not want to turn that lovely hot morning shower into a bootcamp or go to Wim Hoff's extremes, there's room in our travels for the kind of immersive experience that exposure to hot and cold temperatures enables. Whether it's that feeling of the hot desert sands between your toes and the sun shining on your face, or that edifying, skin-tingling, miniscule shock of a moment when you jump from hot water to cold, these sensations provide a heightened physical context where your body is fully immersed in your surrounds. It may well reboot your immune system, and will certainly provide more impetus for mindfully contemplating your here and now.

Top: Arctic Nomad's Greenland experience

Right top: Nubia Desert Camp, Morocco

Right bottom: Blue Lagoon's steaming Icelandic immersion

NOMADIC DESERT TRAVERSE, EGYPT

Sandwiched between the Mediterranean and the Red Sea in Egypt's east, the Sinai Peninsula is the bridge of land between Asia and Africa. Secret Compass' 15-day nomadic camel-ride is a 230-kilometre (143-mile) coast-to-coast journey across Egypt's southern Sinai desert between the Gulfs of Aqaba and Suez. It requires just the bare essentials – you travel with 'little more than the clothes on your back'. You'll be involved with the day-to-day desert tasks of trading camels, bartering with nomads and buying food from the locals on the route. The emphasis is on cultural immersion – this is a chance to feel connected to the heat of the desert and its inhabitants. You'll also enjoy challenges along the way such as climbing several desert peaks including Mount Sinai (2285 metres; 7497 feet) and, Egypt's highest, Mount Catherine (2629 metres; 8625 feet). By night you will sleep under the stars with the comfort of a simple Bedouin blanket to keep you warm in the desert cold. You'll come home wide-eyed with tales of sand-filled wadis, star-splashed night skies, dark-eyed camels and firelit meals.

....

-O- secretcompass.com/expedition/sinai-desert-expedition

THERMAE BATH SPA, BATH, ENGLAND

In the open-air rooftop pool at Thermae Bath Spa, the mineral-rich hot thermal waters sit at the optimum bathing temperature (apparently) of 33.5 degrees Celsius (92.3 degrees Fahrenheit). When this warm water mixes with the cool English temperatures, an atmospheric steam rises into the air lending an otherworldly beauty to the surrounding Gothic pinnacles of Bath Abbey and chimney pots of the city's Georgian architecture. Thermae might be in the middle of Bath's beautiful heritage precinct but the stone- and glass-clad spa and beauty centre is a contemporary ode to an old tradition. Riffing off the city's ancient history as a place where, two millennia ago, Romans and Celts found comfort and solace in bathing rituals, Thermae offers a similarly rejuvenating experience. You can book a two-hour spa session and immerse in the rooftop pool and wellness suites or take it up a notch, choosing one (or more) of the 40 beauty treatments and packages, from the tension relieving 'deep relax hot-stone massage' to the pick-me-up 'reviver facial'. It's so good, you'll want to settle in here for a week.

....

-O- thermaebathspa.com

Top: Thermae Bath Spa, Bath

Bottom: Respite in the Sinai desert

MORNINGTON PENINSULA HOT SPRINGS, VICTORIA, AUSTRALIA

In chilled-out Japan, bathing in hot springs – or onsens – is all part of the culture. In beach-blessed Australia … not so much. But the Mornington Peninsula Hot Springs might be changing that, at least for Victorians. A 75-minute drive from Melbourne's city centre, the spa and wellness sanctuary, set in native bushland, already had a hot springs experience including a bathing gully made up of ten pools, one of them with scenic hilltop views. But the Bath House Amphitheatre, which opened in 2018, boasts seven new geothermal mineral spring pools. The lagoon-shaped natural-looking pools are arranged in an amphitheatre overlooking a tranquil lake and an outdoor stage. Guests can soak in a 38-degree-Celsius (100-degree-Fahrenheit) mineral-rich bath surrounded by trees and birdsong while enjoying open-air musical acts, cultural talks, yoga and other wellbeing classes. In addition, the new bathing area has two cold plunge pools and offers the Fire, Ice and Cave experience, which is based on the idea of cryotherapy. The Ice Cave is kept between 2 and minus 10 degrees Celsius (35 to 14 degrees Fahrenheit) and the Deep Freeze sits on minus 25 degrees Celsius (minus 13 degrees Fahrenheit). With the guidance of an instructor, take the invigorating journey from ice cave and deep freeze to wet and dry saunas, cold plunge, ice plunge and hot spring pools, all the while reading up on the health benefits, which include reduced inflammation, improved sleep quality and increased metabolism.

....

-O- *peninsulahotsprings.com*

The water in these hot springs is unlike any other water on the planet.

BLUE LAGOON, REYKJAVIK, ICELAND

Architecture, design, science and geothermal seawater combine to ensure Iceland's Blue Lagoon is one of the world's most bucket-listed spa experiences. It's located a 30-minute drive from the capital city of Reykjavik within the UNESCO Global Geopark on Reykjanes Peninsula. The peninsula's volcanic provenance ensures the area is a wonderland of geothermal phenomena with craters, fissures, mud pools, steam vents and hot springs. The water in these hot springs is unlike any other water on the planet. It's born in volcanic aquifers 2000 metres (6562 feet) below the Earth's surface where fresh water and ocean water converge 'in a tectonic realm of searing heat and immense pressure'. Blue Lagoon taps into this natural abundance with a series of dreamily blue silica- and sulphur-rich mineral pools surrounded by rugged Icelandic countryside that appears frozen in time. Among the wellness offerings there's a sauna for relaxing in dry heat and a steam cave with an earthen chamber of moist heat. Too hot? Stand beneath the massaging energy of the lagoon waterfall. The luxury Retreat Hotel, opened in 2018, is artfully integrated into the surrounds, allowing guests to delay their inevitable departure with overnight stays.

-O- bluelagoon.com

ALLAS SEA POOL, HELSINKI, FINLAND

The feel-good effects of an icy water swim are no secret to the Finns who enjoy a lifestyle heavily invested in cold-climate activity. In Helsinki's city centre, on a seafront with colourful heritage buildings and a busy market square, Allas Sea Pool is an open-air public pool where anyone can pluck up the courage to dip a toe in the frigid Baltic waters. There are three swimming pools, but it's the sea-water pool – with water pumped in from further out in the ocean – that will test your 'sisu' (the Finnish word meaning something like 'true grit' or mettle). Pack a cap, flip flops and a big fluffy robe or towel ready for your exit and prepare for temperatures that are the same as the Baltic Sea (an average minus 0.3 degrees Celsius, or 31 degrees Fahrenheit, at its coldest in March). Feeling euphoric? That would be the endorphins, the so-called happy hormones released during the cold plunge. Next stop is the sauna, which sits at a sultry 80 degrees Celsius (176 degrees Fahrenheit).

....

-O- allasseapool.fi/en

NUBIA DESERT CAMP, MOROCCO

Just getting to this colourful camp in the dunes of Erg Chegaga, in the Moroccan Sahara, is an adventure. The ancient caravan route from Marrakech is a nine-hour journey through the Berber villages of the Atlas Mountains, past ancient rock formations and into the lush green, palm-striped Draa Valley. Stops include the World Heritage–listed Berber Kasbah town of Ait-Ben-Haddou and the nomadic town of M'hamid El Ghizlane. From here it's a walk or camel trek to the camp, an experience in keeping with the traditions of the local nomadic people. At the Nubia Desert Camp, one of eight handmade Moroccan tents provides a base for discovering the beauty and wonder of the desert. Activities include desert-dune walks to see spectacular views of the Sahara before dining on traditional lamb tagines under the shade of Tamarisk trees (a desert oasis, no less) and sitting fireside on rugs and pillows while listening to traditional Berber music. You can also opt to sleep under the stars.

....

-O- thebeldicollection.com/nubia-luxury-camp

If you're going to leave civilisation behind, this is a good way to go about it. Accessible only via boat or helicopter, secluded Kiattua Camp is located deep in Greenland, in the world's second largest fiord system. On Arctic Nomad Glamping's four-, five- and seven-day packages you'll arrive via an 80-kilometre (50-mile) boat cruise past icebergs and (hopefully) humpback whales. On arrival you'll check in to your own tepee tastefully decked out with a cosy bed, a small table with chairs, and a wood stove to keep you warm at night. Nearby, a separate tent is equipped with hot shower and eco-toilet. When you're all settled in, it's time to get to know the incredible locale. Activities include a short hike to the beautiful waterfall behind the camp with a wow-factor view of the Kiattua Valley and a paddle through the ice in your own kayak with a skilled Inuit guide. You can choose to don a survival suit so as to swim in the Arctic waters and stand on the ice or, depending on your level of fitness, scramble to the summit of the tallest mountain (1650 metres; 5413 feet). Meals from the dining tent are made from freshly sourced local ingredients, from Arctic char and mussels to local mushrooms. End the day with a cleansing body and soul immersion in a hot tub filled with mineral-rich glacial water or take over one of the sauna tents.

ARCTIC NOMAD GLAMPING, NUUK, GREENLAND

....

-O- arctic-nomad.com/kiattua

ELEMENTAL IMMERSION

Sometimes the natural world requires the full attention of our hearts and minds. Other times it demands physical absorption, adrenalin and even a bit of training. Giving yourself over to the wild for a deeper level of connection with the elements is another interpretation of a slow travel experience.

ROCK CLIMBING, OMAN

Two thousand metres (6562 feet) above sea level, Oman's Alila Jabal Akhdar resort is 2.5 hours from Muscat in the dramatic Al Hajar mountain range, home to Jebel Shams, Oman's highest mountain. Views from the eco-conscious stone-and-wood villas and suites take in rugged summits and steep gorges dotted with picturesque abandoned villages, and ravines honeycombed with canyons and caves. The hotel's Via Ferrata (Italian for 'iron path') climbing route, the only one in Oman, begins just a few metres from the hotel below a ridge and takes guests along the mountain face and down a steep section of rock. Not for the faint-hearted, it dares you to defy your innate groundedness by stepping out onto 20-metre-high (66-foot-high) ropes over a cave mouth. Afterwards follow the path down to the village of Al Kutaymi, hidden in a cave in the wadi floor.

-O- alilahotels.com/jabalakhdar

OPEN-WATER SWIMMING, INDONESIA

Indonesia's so-called coral triangle, the marine region near Komodo National Park, is thought to have the planet's highest coral and coral fish diversity and is home to six of the world's seven marine turtles species. Oh, to be among it! Open-water swim tour guru SwimTrek's six-night live-aboard adventure (on an SMY Oceanic yacht) includes a series of swims around the Lesser Sunda Islands, an archipelago with coral-blushed sand beaches, submerged volcanos and crater rims attracting unique sea life. You'll need to be able to swim 5 kilometres (3 miles) in two sections before taking the trip. When you do, this pristine underworld is yours to explore.

-O- swimtrek.com/packages/swimming-holiday-komodo-national-park-indonesia

WHITEWATER RAFTING, USA

With its headwaters in Yosemite National Park, Tuolumne River is considered one of the best in California for rafting with nearly consistent white water. Oars' one-day intermediate-to-advanced rafting trip navigates a beautiful 29-kilometre (18-mile) wilderness canyon. Decked out with helmet, paddle and life vest, you'll encounter hair-raising class IV+ rapids and zip past intricate boulder gardens, rushing cascades and churning holes. The probability that you will become a non-voluntary swimmer is high. Regular exercise for at least three months prior to departure is recommended. A fair price to pay for memories that will last a lifetime.

-O- oars.com/tuolumne-river-itineraries

Top: Open-water swimming, Indonesia
Overleaf: Rock climbing in Oman

GO THE DISTANCE

Ultimate long trips and sabbaticals

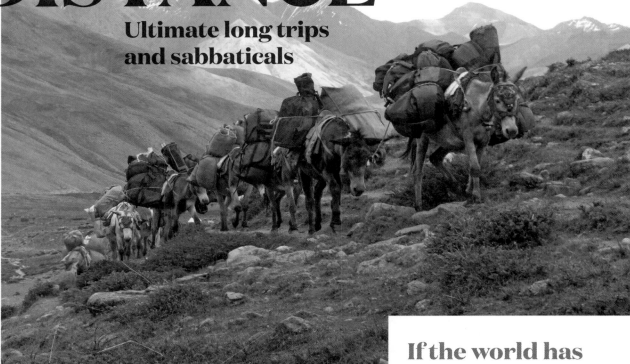

Time has become one of the most valuable commodities on the planet – perhaps it always has been, but in today's hectic world we are finally realising its value. No matter how rich in life's blessings you are, you can still find time wanting. If you are fortunate enough to have plenty of it, you also need to be simultaneously equipped with the skills that will see you use it wisely.

If the world has somehow gifted you time, waste not a minute of this valuable resource.

When I quit the newsroom for a freelance life, my then boyfriend Pip and I decided that if we were going to be working from home, home might as well be anywhere. And why not learn a language while we were at it? With a yearning for Europe, but no plan whatsoever, we pinned the tail on the map and it landed on Andalucía in southern Spain, close to the eye-poppingly beautiful and historic city of Seville. It was a done deal. On landing in London, we bought a jalopy (called Julio) for the roadtrip south through France and Spain. We arrived during the week of the Feria de Abril, the city's biggest festival, and were immediately sold. We rented an apartment just a two-minute walk from the Giralda and enrolled at Don Quijote Spanish School (which proved excellent despite us choosing it for its historic old-town beauty alone). The lifestyle was wonderfully simple. Each day looked something like this: tostado con tomate and café solo, language class, tapas, siesta, language class, tinto de verano (a sacrilegious mix of red wine and lemonade), tapas, sleep, repeat. We didn't get much work done, and we didn't master Spanish exactly, but that year stands out as one of blissful immersion.

If the world has somehow gifted you time (perhaps via a gap year, retirement, redundancy, sabbatical or sheer good luck), waste not a minute of this valuable resource. Find your own way like we did, or sign on to one of these ultimate lifetime adventures and make every second count.

Left and bottom: The characters you meet on the 150-day Great Himalaya Trail

Top: Etosha National Park, Namibia, on the 134-day Western Trans Africa trip

Bordeaux, the name synonymous with some of France's most famous red wines, is also a cultured city boasting notable museums, grand old gardens, cobblestone streets lined with characteristic little bistros and cafes, and the world's largest urban World Heritage site where 18th-century limestone mansions stand next door to Roman ruins. Amid this cosmopolitan loveliness, participants in Road Scholar's 45-day tour can get local on an independent stay and study itinerary. You'll be welcomed by a group leader who will share local customs and culture along with essential practicalities needed for living locally, be it help with public transport passes or directions to the nearest markets and quintessential cafes. On the days following you'll attend expert-led lectures and have hands-on experiences related to your chosen area of study – the region's culinary traditions, wine appreciation or French language skills. Each Friday is cultural day with social events including visits to the Musée des Beaux Arts, wine-tasting at local vineyards, a river cruise and dinner with a local family. On the weekends group field trips go to Saint Jean de Luz, a seaside resort on the Atlantic Coast, and medieval Bayonne. You'll stay in your own hotel apartment in the heart of the city, and check in weekly with your group leader at a cafe.

45 DAYS: LIVING AND LEARNING IN BORDEAUX, FRANCE

....

-O- roadscholar.org/find-an-adventure/23313/living-and-learning-in-bordeaux-independent-stay-and-study

Top: Rue Sainte-Catherine, Bordeaux

Right top: Uyuni Salt Flats, Bolivia

Right bottom: A view on the Great Silk Road Adventure

55 DAYS: ULTIMATE SOUTH AMERICA

How many countries have you been to? If you want to boost your count, this could be the trip for you. Tucan Travel's 55-day itinerary roams most of the South American continent starting in Cartagena in Colombia and weaving down the west coast through Ecuador, Peru, Bolivia and Chile to the southern tip of Argentina before heading up the east coast to Brazil's Rio de Janeiro. You'll also do a side trip to the Galapagos Islands, a biological ark where you can spot sea lions, iguanas and tortoises in the natural habitat that inspired Darwin's theory of evolution. Other boast-worthy activities include walking the Inca Trail to Machu Picchu, floating on Lake Titicaca (the highest navigable lake in the world), setting eyes on the Uyuni Salt Flats and sipping red wine in Argentina.

....

-O- tucantravel.com/tour/ultimate-south-america/hpcr

48 DAYS: GREAT SILK ROAD ADVENTURE, ASIA AND THE MIDDLE EAST

Got some spare time? Will travel? Wild Frontiers' 48-day itinerary along the fabled Silk Road covers an incredible 12,000 kilometres (7456 miles) through six countries. In the footsteps of the ancient silk traders you'll set off from Beijing in China and journey in minibuses, boats, cars, planes and trains through Kyrgyzstan, Uzbekistan, Turkmenistan and Iran to Istanbul in Turkey. En route you'll visit cultural gems such as Xian's Terracotta Army and architectural masterpieces including Samarkand's Registan Square and Istanbul's Blue Mosque. While crossing mountains, deserts and grasslands you'll connect with the people who call these far-off lands their own.

....

-O- wildfrontierstravel.com/en_GB/destination/china/group-tours/master/2001146/the-great-silk-road-adventure-2019

108 DAYS: WORLD ACADEMY CRUISE, GLOBAL

The opulent *Crystal Serenity* cruise ship will be your high-seas home on Road Scholar's 108-day world tour visiting 25 countries. You'll set sail from Miami to Central America, Polynesia, New Zealand, South-East Asia and the Middle East, finally ending in Italy. The trip has an educational theme and your off-shore excursions will be complemented by local expert-led educational programs. Highlights include a local landmarks tour of Mumbai with a history expert and a transit of the Panama Canal where you'll learn about the history of one of the most difficult and dangerous engineering undertakings in the world.

....

-O- roadscholar.org/find-an-adventure/23461/road-scholar-world-academy-around-the-world-in-style

134 DAYS: WESTERN TRANS AFRICA FROM DAKAR TO CAPE TOWN

Epic is the word. Dragoman's 134-day adventure begins in the western-most part of mainland Africa and takes a slow overland route through some of Africa's least visited countries to Cape Town on the southern tip of the continent. It's touted as 'a long unpredictable and hard journey' where adventurous guests (who may be well out of their comfort zone) should 'expect the unexpected and embrace it'. Love it! You'll visit 17 countries including Senegal, Gambia, Guinea, the Ivory Coast, Ghana, Togo, Benin and Nigeria. Highlights include wild camping in local villages en route, a two-day overland safari through Etosha National Park, relaxing on the beaches of Freetown Peninsula in Sierra Leone, and visiting Tiwai Island Wildlife Sanctuary in the hope of spotting a rare pygmy hippo.

....

-O- dragoman.com/holidays/details/western-trans-africa-sahel-to-the-cape

Top: Cape Town, on the challenging Western Trans Africa trip

Left: The Crystal Serenity *cruises the world*

150 DAYS: GREAT HIMALAYAN TRAIL

Stories of determination, achievement and personal growth are the by-product of this truly epic 1700-kilometre (1056-mile) trek along the world's highest and longest alpine walking route, known as the Great Himalayan Trail. Exclusive to World Expeditions, the 150-day adventure follows the lead of only a handful of trekkers who have, over the past decade, completed the walk, ticking off all eight of Nepal's 8000-metre (26,000-foot) peaks along the way. Beginning in Nepal's far east you'll navigate through remote villages, high mountain passes and rarely visited valleys in the high plateaus on the far-west Tibetan borderlands. Himalayan vistas are a sight you will never weary of. The trail can also be completed individually in seven treks.

....

-O- trekthegreathimalayatrail.com

365 DAYS: ULTIMATE AROUND THE WORLD WELLNESS TRIP, GLOBAL

Described as the long-term answer to Sunday evening meltdowns and cases of Mondayitis, Health and Fitness Travel's 365-day trip around the globe is a life-changer no matter which way you look at it. The 20-country itinerary has a healthy lifestyle theme and promises 'educational health consultations, inspiring fitness training, healing spa therapies and healthy nutrition'. In essence, you'll kick the bad habits while tripping around some of the world's most luxurious resorts, decadent spas and holistic habitats. The trip includes a hike along Australia's Great Ocean Walk, yoga and meditation in the southern Alps of New Zealand, optimal wellbeing at a medical spa in Brazil, luxury wellness at a retreat on Turkey's Aegean coast, and a Buddhist temple immersion in Thailand. Six-month trips are also available.

....

-O- healthandfitnesstravel.com/ultimate-worldwide-
   wellness-trip-one-year

Top: The epic Great Himalayan Trail

Right: Apo Island in the Philippines is a stop on the year-long Wellness Trip

Round-the-world yachtie

When Matt Hayes was 18 he had an experience that could have seen him give up sailing for good. He was on a night race on a small yacht called *Montego Bay* sailing from Sydney Harbour to Port Hacking. The weather was against them and as the storm set in along the coast near Bondi it became obvious that the boat was going to sink. Everyone leapt overboard with the exception of one guy who went downstairs to send a mayday call. In the water, Hayes found an esky and he and the skipper stayed afloat for five or six hours with no lifejackets. Eventually, a boat came past and picked them up. They found out later that the crew member who had gone downstairs to call mayday had drowned, and that three members of another yacht that sank that night also died. It was one of the worse nautical losses of life in Australia in peacetime.

INTERVIEW:

Matt Hayes

Overleaf: Tanah Lot temple, in Bali, is a highlight on the 108-day global cruise (see p. 32)

This tragedy made a huge impression on Hayes – he realised that life is short and we should grab onto it with both hands. Despite the experience, he continued sailing and also became a strong ocean swimmer. He went on to represent Australia in sailing at the 1996 Olympic Games in Atlanta and has since competed all over the world. When I caught up with the Sydneysider for a chat via email, he was halfway through a World ARC (worldcruising.com) round-the-world yachting rally, a 26,000-nautical-mile trade-wind circumnavigation. In other words, a voyage of a lifetime.

What have been your biggest challenges thus far?
There have been many. Boat preparation. The sheer volume of boat maintenance. Living in a small space with other people without escape and dealing with the incredible amount of organisation required.

What have been the biggest surprises?
As we are doing a rally with 19 other yachts, it can be a bit like *Days of Our Lives*. Many wonderful people, likeminded, friendly, caring and always looking out for each other both at sea and on land. How accurate weather forecasting actually is. How many flying fish end up on deck.

Moments of sheer joy?
Swimming with whale sharks at St Helena. Walking though the only human-made cloud forest in Ascension Island. Sailing into Mauritius after a rough 2500-nautical-mile passage across the Indian Ocean. Leaving Sydney among fanfare. Being surrounded by around 100 seals off Namibia. A helicopter tour around the Cirques of Reunion Island. Diving with tortoises at Ascension.

Moments of pain?
Losing a yacht tender and an outboard motor – they were washed away. Breaking some gear and ripping a sail.

Best slow travel moment?
At night, on deck on my own in the South Atlantic, stars everywhere, gentle rolling seas, calm winds, peace and quiet, fresh air and time to think about life's wonders.

Moments of fear?
Walking around Durban City. Misinterpreting a cyclone heading our way. Waking at night to find a crew member steering the boat 35 degrees off course and heading for a beach.

What physical and mental challenges have come from the journey so far?
Physical challenges include continuing to stay fit (I swam a lot at home). You are always active at sea – there is heavy lifting, winching, climbing and so on – but you only get good exercise on shore. Mental challenges include staying focused and continuing to understand the importance of fast-track learning.

Has such an extended journey changed the way you look and feel about the natural world?
Yes! One hundred per cent. We need to focus on doing everything possible to look after endangered species – for example, orangutans are on the critically endangered list and could be extinct in a decade. And I am much more aware about the pressing need to get rid of plastic after seeing the enormous amount of it littering Indonesia, and washing up in pristine places such as the Cocos (Keeling) Islands. Mother Nature, flora, fauna and native animals all need a voice.

And lastly, what advice would you give to someone keen to take on a similar journey?
Ask yourself this question: when is the right time? Is it waiting for more money? For the stock market to pick up or property prices to bounce back? Should you wait until retirement? The answer is there is no perfect time. There is only now and you may as well just do it now.

ANIMAL INSTINCT

Journeys into animal habitats

When people ask me to name my best ever trip, it's a tough one, but an expedition up to the icy, remote yet entirely awesome Canadian town of Churchill, in Manitoba, to see polar bears prowling around their wild environs always comes somewhere in my top three. The completely alien landscape (you can't get further removed from what I'm used to in Melbourne) was a major part of the attraction, but the real clincher was the immersion in an animal habitat. There's something totally enlivening about putting aside your own wants, needs, thoughts even, to tune into the natural world. Just sitting there, watching and waiting, taking mental notes, being attuned to the slightest change, is a lesson in curiosity and an investment in slow. A ream of research suggests that the companionship of pets has meaningful life benefits. Extrapolating on that fact, I'm convinced the animal world has similar benefits for travellers, as long as we keep our respectful distance. If we're protecting or helping them, even better.

Top: A lone wolf on the Mystical Transylvania research expedition

Right top: Zebras on Ulwazi's research programme in South Africa

Right bottom: Polar bears on the icy tundra adventure in Canada

SNOW LEOPARD EXPEDITION, INDIA

Northern India's Trans-Himalayan region of Ladakh, known as Little Tibet, is one of the last frontiers for wildlife tourism. The high altitude region is all big skies, dramatic snow-capped mountain crags and open plains, and the traditional villages sport Buddhist temples and folk wearing traditional stove-pipe hats and felt boots with turned up toes. On this 13-day journey, operated by AndBeyond, a maximum of eight guests will be led in search of Asia's sleek and soulful snow leopard, dubbed the mountain ghost for its elusive manner and camouflaged coat. In Ulley, relatively free of tourism, you'll stay seven nights at Snow Leopard Lodge with a Ladakhi family and explore three valleys in search of the elusive creature. Keep the binoculars out for other native wonders including wolf, Himalayan fox and male horned ibex, which are a picture when they stand vigil on impossibly rocky outcrops. The trip includes a visit to the Snow Leopard Conservancy to learn about the efforts of local authorities and communities in conserving this endangered species.

....

-O- andbeyond.com/small-group-journeys/snow-leopard

CHURCHILL POLAR BEARS, CANADA

Churchill is way north of Winnipeg on the icy shores of Hudson Bay. There are no roads – it's accessible by an overnight train (just back on track after being closed for repairs for two years) or a small plane, which touches down on an icy tarmac dotted with 'Beware: Polar Bear' signs. The main action happens 16 kilometres (10 miles) out of town on the tundra: a permafrost landscape, whipped by Arctic winds, is the seasonal meeting place for the bears waiting for Hudson Bay to freeze over so they can go hunting for ringed seal. On Frontiers North's five-day itinerary, you'll watch male polar bears sparring and cute cubs playing in the snow from one of the purpose-built tundra buggies, which are kitted out to protect the environment while keeping guests comfortable. Depending on which tour you choose, guests sleep and eat in the tundra buggy lodge or, my pick, at a hotel in Churchill where you can learn about polar bear conservation, interact with the local Inuit community and get a taste for how quirky this place is. Keep an eye to the sky for the aurora borealis.

....

-O- frontiersnorth.com/adventures/churchill-town-and-tundra-adventurer

ULWAZI RESEARCH PROGRAMME, SOUTH AFRICA

On a 140-square-kilometre (54-square-mile) private game reserve in South Africa's KwaZulu-Natal province, you can stay in luxurious Thanda Safari lodge, exclusive Villa iZulu or Thanda Tented Camp for a wild Big Five safari experience. Better still, you can use up the long-service leave by signing up for a two- to four-week stay at the property's Ulwazi, a conservation research program. In the early 2000s, when Thanda Safari was established, all the naturally occurring wildlife species that had historically lived here were reintroduced. Since then, it has been proclaimed a Protected Environment within South Africa's Biodiversity Stewardship Programme. Stay in the rustic safari-style thatched chalets of Thanda Safari's Intibane Research and Training Centre and immerse yourself into projects such as the Hyena Population Density and Space Utilisation project, or the Nocturnal Animal Survey. The latter was set up to gain greater understanding and knowledge of the aardvark, honey badger, leopard, white-tailed mongoose and serval, and requires combining data from camera traps with data from night-drive monitoring. You'll also learn about the day-to-day management of the reserve, including the monitoring of endangered species, and habitat management involving practical field data collection and analysis. You'll get to know the neighbouring Zulu communities who are part of Thanda Safari's wildlife and management teams. Ulwazi means place of learning in isiZulu. That says it all.

....

-O- *ulwaziresearch.com*

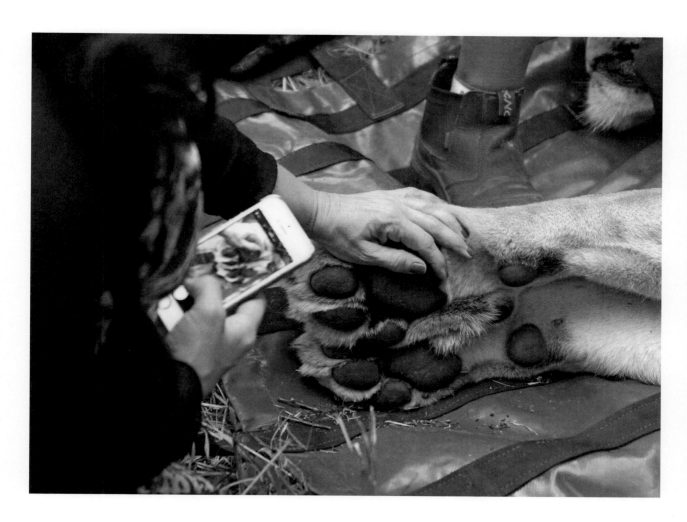

KAYAKING WITH ORCAS, CANADA

This rugged coastline is blanketed with west-coast rainforest, home to black bears and bald eagles.

During the Canadian summer, in the cool clear waters of Johnstone Strait off Vancouver Island, orcas congregate to feed, socialise and rub themselves on pebble beaches. For kayakers, it's a chance to see these magnificent mammals up close in their native environment. Spotting a spouting orca pod or a gleaming ebony-black dorsal fin slicing the water will make your day; seeing one breach is a memory of a lifetime. The seven-day trip, operated by World Expeditions, is a true British Columbia immersion. On water you'll explore coves and beaches, keeping an eye out for other marine life including seals, sea lions, dolphins, porpoises and the occasional humpback, minke or grey whale. There's plenty to see on land too. This rugged coastline is blanketed with west-coast rainforest, home to black bears and bald eagles. At night, while camping, you'll also have your eyes to the skies – the clear nights and zero light pollution make this prime country for stargazing.

....

-O- *worldexpeditions.com/Canada/Raft-Canoe-Kayak/ Kayaking-with-Orcas*

MYSTICAL TRANSYLVANIA (WITHOUT THE VAMPIRES), ROMANIA

The mountains, cliffs, meadows and forests of the Carpathian Mountains in Romania's fabled Transylvanian Alps are the terrain for this citizen-science research expedition. Organised by Biosphere Expeditions, the mission is to undertake conservation research on bear, wolf, lynx, bison and beaver species, as well as their interrelationships with prey species and humans. By night you'll stay in the expedition base, a comfortable chalet with all modern amenities. By day you'll track and study these animals in a 360-square-kilometre (139-square-mile) zone. Activities include placing and checking camera traps, learning how to collect samples of scat and fur for genetic analysis, and surveying prey species such as deer and wild boar. You don't need to be a scientist or have any special qualifications, just the ability to walk about 10 to 20 kilometres (6 to 12 miles) per day in hilly to mountainous terrain in autumn conditions. The end game? Be part of the creation of a world-class wilderness reserve and a new national park, which will be among Europe's biggest. Now, that's something for your résumé.

....

-O- *biosphere-expeditions.org/volunteeringinromania*

HORSING AROUND

From the elevated saddle of a horse you can see the world from a different perspective. Whether you're trotting, galloping or cantering, these equine adventures offer a chance to cover new terrain on four legs.

BIG GAME PARKS TRAIL, ESWATINI (SWAZILAND)

Chubeka Trails' latest venture is a 10-day itinerary including a six-day horse-trail and three-day safari through the changing habitats of Eswatini's three Big Game Parks. It begins at Mlilwane Wildlife Sanctuary and traverses the infamous Nyonyane Mountain, trekking over exciting river crossings, through rural Swazi Nation Land communities, and into the uninhabited mountains of Mlilwane North for brilliant views across South Africa, Eswatini and Mozambique. The trip includes three nights camping in bell tents.

....
-O- biggameparks.org/properties/chubeka-trails-6

HORSING AROUND, ANDALUCÍA, SPAIN

A beautiful whitewashed Spanish hacienda and Andalucía's olive groves, oak and cork forests, sunflower fields and pine copses set the scene for Original Travel's four-day Horsing Around itinerary, which is designed to balance Andalucían hospitality and culture with horseback time. The family-owned country house has tastefully rustic rooms set around a cobbled courtyard along with three swimming pools, a small tennis court, a library and an honesty bar. You'll have the chance for a good gallop on two morning horserides that are nicely rounded-off with al fresco lunches in the countryside. The itinerary also includes a guided tour of Seville with its Moorish palaces and tapas bars, then a visit to some of the region's charming pueblos blancos (whitewashed towns) that top the hills and sierras of the region.

....
-O- originaltravel.co.uk/itineraries/horsing-around-andalucia

ZAVKHAN CLASSIC TREK, MONGOLIA

Zavkhan Province is difficult to get to with its erratic flights and challenging roads. On the upside, there are no tourists and it's perfect riding terrain. This 17-day journey starts with a roadtrip to Zavkhan to meet the horses. From there it's nine to ten days of riding across the open steppe, through forested valleys, and up into the mountains of Tarvagatai Nuruu National Park meeting nomadic herdspeople along the way. You'll then head either south to Khar Nuur, a desert lake with sand dunes on its edge, or north to remote Gandan Nuur to hike, swim and relax, saddle-sore but happy, around an atmospheric lake.

....
-O- zavkhan.co.uk

Left: A rest point while kayaking with orcas in Canada (see p. 42)

Top: Horsing around in Andalucía, Spain

Overleaf: Riding through Zavkhan Province, Mongolia

BETTER ME

Wellness retreats and resorts

While travel health and wellbeing were once confined to often-exclusive retreats, nowadays wellness experiences are a mainstay of most resort and hotel offerings. You can rise early for a poolside yoga class, eat from menus with little healthy option symbols and add a holistic treatment to your line-up of spa treatments. And while yoga retreats are now almost mainstream, wellness adventures — trips specifically mapped out with wellness-focused itineraries — are the next big thing.

My first moment of pure wellness occurred in Bhutan while relaxing in a wooden hot tub awaiting a hot-stone massage. I had just hiked to Tiger's Nest Monastery, that iconic temple teetering on the edge of a mountain cliff. I was exhausted from the experience but culturally enlightened, spiritually awakened, physically fulfilled and now — while sitting in warm water heated by hot rocks from a local stream — mentally rejuvenated. I was tapping into mindfulness, though I didn't know it then. This nexus of mind, body, spirit and an overwhelming sense of fulfillment is what wellness is all about and slow travel provides the means of getting there.

Top: The Farm at San Benito in the Philippines

Right top: New Zealand scenery from the pool at Aro Hā retreat

Right bottom: Mozambique's eye-wateringly beautiful Azura Quilalea resort

RETREATS

For total immersion, these retreats offer holistic, natural and medicinal pathways to healing your body, mind and spirit. Exotic locations and luxurious hospitality are added bonuses.

ARO HĀ, NEW ZEALAND

In the rarefied air of New Zealand's Southern Alps, 40 minutes from Queenstown, Aro Hā is all about breathing and B.R.E.A.T.H: being, relating, eating, activity, toxicity, healing. At this intensive wellness haven, these elements are addressed through a fusion of Zen-styled eco-accommodation, self-sufficient permaculture practices and a program that encourages rejuvenation of the human spirit. On a retreat here, you'll enjoy vegetarian cuisine (Paleo friendly, gluten free, dairy free and enzymatically active), healing bodywork and daily mindfulness practice. This is combined with subalpine hiking, vinyasa yoga and dynamic movement. The six-day itinerary usually starts with a sunrise flow yoga class, energising breakfast and hike into the World Heritage–listed mountainous surrounds. After a 'nutrient-dense' lunch, the pace changes. You can indulge in rejuvenation and spa time, a massage, strength training and a nutrition demo. At the end of each day, relax with a restorative yoga class, mindfulness session, leisurely dinner and even some journalling time. The end result is returning to the real world with a still mind and an energised body.

Aro Hā is all about breathing and B.R.E.A.T.H: being, relating, eating, activity, toxicity, healing.

....

-O- aro-ha.com

THE FARM AT SAN BENITO, THE PHILIPPINES

Lush tropical jungle and mountain views set the scene at this eco-luxury resort in Lipa, Batangas, 90 minutes south of Manila. Known throughout South-East Asia for combining traditional healing techniques with integrative medicine, the Farm's 'healing retreats' start with detox cleansing, wellness spa treatments and organic vegan food alongside yoga, meditation and a fitness regimen. In addition, with fully trained integrative medical doctors, nurses, spa therapists and nutritionists on hand, guests can sign up for personalised natural and holistic health programs that deal with common fast-world ailments such as diabetes, obesity, hypertension, stress and depression. Mind you, it feels more like a tropical resort than a clinic. Treehouse-style suites and villas sit among palm-fronded greenery and the recliner-busy swimming pool is sweetly scented by frangipani trees. There are group walks in the morning and tai chi classes in the afternoon, and the spa offers Hilot massage, an ancient Filipino healing technique.

-O- *thefarmatsanbenito.com*

COMO SHAMBHALA ESTATE, INDONESIA

Remember in Elizabeth Gilbert's book *Eat, Pray, Love* when the protagonist travels to Bali to find inner peace and healing? Well, Bali's Como Shambhala Estate offers something similar, if not a little more luxurious. Sitting above the Ayung River, near Ubud, amid verdant fruit trees, exotic flowers and vine-covered palms, Como Shambhala is as close to an earthly paradise as it gets. Opened in 1997, the Como flagship retreat has long been into body, mind and soul, offering organic cuisine and Pilates and yoga classes long before they became on-trend in the West. You can put the pressures of the modern world on hold with all-inclusive packages that include massage and bodywork, spa treatments, intuitive counselling and ancient healing therapies, such as Ayurveda, an Indian healing system. When not building a better self, simply enjoy the serenity. Shambhala refers to 'a sacred place of bliss' and this wonderful place achieves it. There are natural spring-fed pools, suites and villas adorned with Balinese teak furnishings, and a forest filled with rambutan, durian and white mango trees. Heaven on Earth.

-O- *comohotels.com/en/comoshambhalaestate*

EUPHORIA RETREAT, GREECE

Mount Taygetos, rising 2407 metres (7897 feet) above sea level, is the tallest mountain in the Greek Peloponnese and Euphoria Retreat is built into its rocky mountainside. The four-storey wellness haven's beautiful rock walls and terracotta rooftops blend seamlessly with the native fir and pine trees. 'Euphoria' in its original Greek translates as 'a state of happiness and bliss' and this new holistic wellbeing destination hits the mark. The hybrid East–West wellness ideals fuse ancient Taoist and Hellenic philosophies with Chinese and Hippocratic medicine. In short, the wellbeing program revolves around earth, fire, water, wood and metal to address emotional, physical and spiritual health. You can come here for day visits, but the seven-day signature intensive retreat, the Euphoria Emotional and Physical Transformation, is the standout: a three-step approach to soul cleansing combining exercise, nutrition and mental coaching with energy balancing treatments, nutrition and group therapies. If you have the inner stamina, activities and workshops include wellness lectures, nutrition classes, meditation, yoga, Qi Gong and Pilates. There's a dreamy pool with an opening in the rock wall so you can swim from indoors to outside. Time-out on the sun-deck is another must. Beyond the citrus groves, olive trees and modern town of Sparta is the fortified town of Mystras, a World Heritage site with Byzantine churches, palaces and fortresses

....

-O- *euphoriaretreat.com/en*

RESORTS

Not everybody wants to forgo life's cheeky pleasures while travelling. In fact, many of us regard Bacchanalian eating and drinking and lazing poolside as integral to a recharge. Happily, today's resorts cater to many moods, combining all the gay abandon of a vacation with some well-placed self-betterment thrown in. In this ever-evolving slow travel landscape, resorts and hotels are offering wellness that connects nicely with the surrounding destination, providing a seamless blend of travel, indulgence and immersion.

Top: Me-time at Azura Quilalea resort in Mozambique

Bottom: Swimming explorations at Thailand's Trisara resort

TRISARA, THAILAND

Trisara resort, on the mountainous tropical island of Phuket, sits so close to the Andaman Sea it's almost possible – at a stretch during high tide – to dangle your fingers in the infinity pool while tickling your toes in the ocean waves. The gentle rhythms of Thai life are evoked in this serene environment – each villa has sea views, a private swimming pool, large teak beds, ceiling fans and outdoor showers surrounded by tropical gardens. The beauty spa has wellness packages with treatments and yoga sessions that you can tap into at leisure over the course of your stay. But the highlight is PRU, the resort's degustation restaurant and the first Phuket restaurant to be awarded a Michelin star. The restaurant has turned its gaze away from the dazzle of the ocean to focus inland on sustainable farm-to-table dining from Phuket's own terroir (PRU stands for plant, raise, understand). It sources 100 per cent of produce from within Thailand and 75 per cent from Phuket, much of it from the resort's own farm and wild garden where foraged ingredients – sweet fruits and sour leaves – give each dish distinctive Thai flavours. The dishes all have neat little backstories about their island origins: carrot (the best carrot I have ever tasted) is baked underground for six hours and served with a fermented carrot juice hollandaise; the wagyu beef is sourced from a Thai farmer; fresh-picked rosella leaves make perfect sorbet. It's wellness worth eating.

....

-O- *trisara.com*

AZURA QUILALEA, MOZAMBIQUE

Eye-wateringly blue water and swathes of white sand underscore the remoteness of this pristine private island, part of Mozambique's Indian Ocean Quirimbas Archipelago. This is castaway island stuff, albeit with a big fat dose of luxury. Nine seafront villas have thatched roofs, natural wood furnishings and earthy tones that set off the sparkling blue of private swimming pools. The uninhabited (by humans) island is mostly jungle, alive with boab trees and migratory bird species, while the surrounding water – fit for snorkelling, kayaking and swimming – is designated marine sanctuary. The Azura's new 'hyperconsciousness' wellness program 'Sounds of Africa' aims to immerse guests in this environment by focusing on the sights, smells, sounds and tastes of Africa. It features African drumming therapy – a tribal combination of singing, meditation, exercise and rhythm to promote healing and self-expression; and mindful walking meditation, where guests are guided around the island and encouraged to tune in to the sounds of nature – the call of a black sunbird here, the song of a dark-capped bulbul there. Paying more mindful attention to the environment has various benefits including reducing anxiety and improving cognition – a win-win on holiday.

....

-O- *azura-retreats.com*

BELMOND MOUNT NELSON HOTEL, SOUTH AFRICA

There's no escaping Cape Town's Table Mountain at this indulgent hotel sitting pretty in pink (literally) at its base. Surrounded by a beautiful garden, the hotel has close to 200 rooms and suites, two swimming pools, the same number of tennis courts and a kids' club. If you want more than just glimpses of the iconic flat-topped mountain, the hotel offers dawn walks – you'll take a pair of high-definition binoculars to encounter the captivating flora and fauna of Table Mountain in truly magical morning light. Also on offer are painting classes, hosted by talented local painter Cyril Coetzee, and, best of all, a Table Mountain yoga class. You'll be collected from the hotel and escorted to the cable-car station, where your instructor joins you for the early morning ride up. On this monument of Mother Nature, you'll partake in a 60-minute class overlooking Cape Town and the Southern Ocean – sun salutations par excellence.

....

-O- belmond.com/hotels/africa/south-africa/cape-town/
belmond-mount-nelson-hotel

You'll be collected from the hotel and escorted to the cable-car station, where your instructor joins you for the early morning ride up.

TRANSFORM

The tour group experience is ever-changing. Its latest evolution – in-depth wellness experiences – sees tour groups combining awe-inspiring activities and sightseeing with opportunities to enliven the mind, body and soul. It's a chance to reconnect with yourself and the planet by getting the balance between travelling and slowing down just right.

WELLNESS JOURNEY, COSTA RICA

Like a good yoga class, this eight-day G Adventures tour starts in San Jose where you set your intentions for the trip – then the journey really begins. The first feel-good stop is to sample the beans at Mi Cafecito Community Coffee cooperative, a G Adventures project supporting 200 local farmers and their families. Next is La Fortuna, an outdoor utopia where you'll stretch into a yoga session overlooking the Arenal Volcano. On day three, you're up and at 'em with a stand-up paddleboard yoga class (yes, it's possible), followed by your choice of hiking, canyoning, rest or meditation. In the evening, rejuvenate your muscles, detox your cells and stimulate all your senses with a hot springs soak. Another highlight is Rincón de la Vieja, a lush jungle environment where sulphuric ponds filled with mud bubble next to volcanic thermal waters. You'll take a therapeutic bath here before another yoga class for full invigoration. The final three days are based around the beach in Playa Carrillo with sand-footed beach yoga classes and sure-footed surf lessons. Then it's time to take the new you back to San Jose.

....

-O- gadventures.com.au/trips/wellness-costa-rica/
CRSSW

Top left: Prayer flags fluttering in Bhutan
Top right: A meditative walk in La Fortuna, Costa Rica

DILLY BAG TOUR FOR WOMEN, AUSTRALIA

Australian Indigenous tourism operator Lirrwi Tourism's itineraries of the Yolngu Homelands in the Northern Territory's East Arnhem Land includes the Dilly Bag Tour for Women. The 'dilly bag', known as gay'wu in the local language, is an important and powerful cultural symbol in its homeland of Arnhem Land, where it was first created thousands of years ago. Woven with dyed pandanus leaves, the dilly bag is significant both for its practicality in carrying bush foods and medicines, and for its spiritual meaning as a carrier of knowledge. Developed by Yolngu traditional owners, with multiple family generations participating, this five-day tour will immerse you in Indigenous culture, connecting you with Yolngu women and their land. You'll learn about their culture, history and country through activities such as weaving, painting, healing and crying ceremonies (Nathi), cooking, bush medicine, dancing and oyster gathering. These traditionally female experiences will help connect you with Yolngu people environmentally, spiritually and philosophically.

....

-O- lirrwitourism.com.au/womens-tours

HIMALAYAN EXPLORER, BHUTAN

The hot-stone bath treatment (known as a dotsho) on this trip is my kind of utopia, but the locals have bigger ideas. Bhutan, a landlocked Himalayan country, is a proudly Buddhist country with an official Gross National Happiness index. In the stupas and dzongs (fortresses) that dot the mountains and valleys, thousands of monks count beads and spin prayer wheels in anticipation of a heavenly Buddhist afterlife. In the capital of Thimphu, the fifth ruling king is keen on the idea of an earthly social paradise where happiness is more important than gross domestic product. He has eased his people seamlessly into the 21st century on this premise so that they ooze the kind of contentment that makes travelling here feel like a quest for happiness. Como Hotel's five-day Himalayan Explorer itinerary explores Bhutan's cultures and traditions with visits to ancient dzongs, temples and museums and – the highlight – a 5-kilometre (3-mile) hike to spectacular Tiger's Nest Monastery, a red-and-gold-roofed temple clinging to a sheer cliff face 900 metres (2953 feet) above the Paro Valley. Inside, outrageously colourful shrines tell the stories of mythical creatures and historical figures. After a sweaty five-hour journey, that hot-stone bath really proves its worth – happiness guaranteed.

....

-O- comohotels.com/en/umaparo/offers/himalayan-explorer

WELLNESS FESTIVALS

Move over music festivals, the global stage is big enough for wellness festivals too. Where decibels, all-nighters and hangovers once reigned, the interest in clean living has seen a jump in the number of wellness festivals. Slow travellers can now combine wanderlust and wellness at global feel-good fests, from a healing workshop at BaliSpirit Festival in Indonesia to a hip-hop yoga session at Soul Circus in England.

BALISPIRIT FESTIVAL, INDONESIA

The BaliSpirit Festival, held in March each year, embodies the core mantra of Balinese Hinduism, which is to live in harmony with spiritual, social and natural environments. But it's also a yoga, dance and music fest. Surrounded by lush green foliage, sacred trees and rice fields, you can choose from interactive workshops, seminars, yoga, dance, healing and world music, and a lively community market and healing centre. Devotional Bhakti music concerts will bring the night-time to life.

....

-O- balispiritfestival.com

WONDERFRUIT, THAILAND

Start the Asian summer at Wonderfruit festival. This weekend celebration of the arts, held in December each year, aims to recharge mind, body and soul through live music, artfully cooked authentic Thai food, performance art and innovation in sustainability. It's held at the Siam Country Club in Pattaya, Thailand, and features more than 100 activities under the Wonder Garden program. The festival organisers use recycled materials to construct its stages and public spaces, and you won't see any single-use straws or plastic plates.

....

-O- wonderfruit.co

MOUNTAIN YOGA FESTIVAL, AUSTRIA

The fresh air, forests and meadows of St Anton are as much a part of this festival as the yoga poses. Held in September each year in the alpine village of St Anton am Arlberg in Austria, the festival attracts international teachers, yogis and nature lovers keen to salute to the sun surrounded by blue skies, green fields and craggy mountains. The four-day program incorporates mountain and village yoga sessions with a hiking tour, morning meditations, yoga talks and a music night.

⌀ mountainyogafestivalstanton.at

SOUL CIRCUS, COTSWOLDS, ENGLAND

The Cotswolds is at its best during the British summer, when the lavender is in bloom and the sun is (mostly) shining. In mid-August Soul Circus takes full advantage with a three-day spiritual wellness festival. With more than 250 classes and 100 international big-name 'soul teachers', it's the ultimate yogi fest with a difference. Participants can take on a hip-hop yoga class (which will have you 'twerking your down dog' according to the festival), aerial yoga using silks and hoops 6 metres (20 feet) above the ground, or AcroYogaDance, a partner yoga practice. There are also mindful crafts, activities such as life-drawing and journalling workshops, a stage for live music, a soul cafe and a cocktail bar.

⌀ soulcircus.yoga

WELLFEST, DUBLIN, IRELAND

One of Europe's biggest health and fitness events, Wellfest is held in May each year at the Royal Hospital Kilmainham in Dublin. It attracts more than 150 wellness experts including fitness and yoga specialists, psychology and mindfulness practitioners, talented foodies and qualified nutritionists. There are 15 stages so you can handpick from the line-up of classes, workshops and seminars to suit your wellness needs without any limitations. Headliners in 2019 included Fearne Cotton, Brit author of podcast series Happy Place, and Amanda Bisk, elite Aussie pole vaulter turned yoga and fitness expert.

⌀ wellfest.ie

Opposite left and right: Faces from the Balispirit Festival, Indonesia

Top: Mountain yoga in Austria

Bottom: Fun at Soul Circus in the Cotswolds

Overleaf: Indoor–outdoor swimming at Euphoria Retreat in Greece (see p. 52)

TWO FEET

Walking and hiking

'Every. Single. Step. Hurts. Like. Hell. But (deep breath) there's no turning back. Up front, leading the charge like a pair of over-zealous explorers are my energetic future in-laws and (another breath) I've promised (myself mainly) not to complain at least until much later, when my muscles are recovering in a warm bath (sigh) and the in-laws are well out of earshot.'

Or so I wrote a number of years ago in a travel article about my first real walking experience. We were climbing – 'slow, steady and in single file' – up to High Cup Nick, one of the many walks crisscrossing the northern Pennines near Appleby in England's ancient county of Westmorland. The Pennines is a mountain range extending from just north of the Scottish border south to the foothills of Derbyshire in the Midlands. Like the country's famous Coast to Coast walk, the 431-kilometre (268-mile) Pennine Way National Trail is one of the most demanding in Britain and something of a rite of passage for serious walkers. Which raised the question in my story back then: 'What am I doing climbing even just a small section of it?'

My answer was a matter of self-preservation: 'If I'm to spend a lifetime of Christmas holidays with my new English family, then I'm going to have to cultivate an interest in walking. As I'm fast discovering, it's a very English thing to do.'

The answer now would be quite different, but the end game is the same. After a few years of walking with the in-laws, be it on leisurely strolls with dogs trailing behind, or on far-flung hikes, I now seek out this slow activity. The fresh air, the me-time, the one-foot-after-the-other meditation and the quiet immersion in the places around you are addictive. I now add small walks and hikes to travel itineraries, where possible, to get a sense of the natural landscape or to find an escape from the hustle and bustle. My partner and I often talk about completing that Coast to Coast walk, along with many others – the Camino de Santiago in Spain, the Jatbula Trail in Australia's Northern Territory … the list goes on.

Walks, hikes and treks in all their different forms are a slow experience you can rely on the world over, be it on a blistering month-long cross-country odyssey or an afternoon escapade up a nearby hill. It's possibly the purest form of slow travel because you're right in the heart of the action, planting one foot after the other while absorbing the minutiae and detail in every footfall. When employing two feet and a heartbeat you're breathing, you're listening, you're tuning into the world around you – like mindfulness on legs. You're also likely to be taking better photos and perhaps more notice of your walking buddies. You're undoubtedly uncovering nature's little secrets – birds, bees, buds, blooms, the little things that go unacknowledged at a faster pace.

It's possibly the purest form of slow travel because you're right in the heart of the action ...

Left: Snow-kissed mountains on the Banff hike in Canada

Top: Lofty highs on the walk through the Appalachians and New England

KUMANO KODO, JAPAN

Ready for a spiritual immersion? The Kii Peninsula is one of Japan's most enigmatic and mystical regions, and it's here you'll find the crisscrossing ancient mountainous trails of the Kumano Kodo pilgrimage network. On Inside Japan's five-night self-guided hiking adventure, you'll navigate difficult but rewarding terrain trodden by pilgrims from all walks of life for over a thousand years. Stride through great swathes of untouched forest and past Hongu Taisha and Nachi Taisha, two of the three great shrines known collectively as the Kumano Sanzan (the third is Hayatama Taisha). This five-night itinerary is a mainstream trail but it packs in some of the more challenging sections of the Kumano Kodo between Kii-Tanabe and Kii-Katsuura. Good walking boots are essential. In the villages of Nonaka and Koguchi, you'll stay at traditional Japanese inns — the kind with impeccable service, futons, tatami mat floors and sliding screen walls. In Yunomine, the famous onsen town, you can bathe your weary bones in Japan's only World Heritage–listed hot springs bath. Features of the route include the remains of the Uwada-jaya Teahouse (the highest part of this trail at 690 metres (2264 feet) above sea level) and the giant Nonaka-no-Ipposugi cedar trees of Tsugizakura-oji Shrine. Little extras include an informative guide on the first day, delicious kaiseki dinners and chef-cooked packed lunches for your backpack.

64

-O- insidejapantours.com/self-guided-
japan-holidays/i-kk002/kumano-kodo-
five-night-module-advanced-hiking-

MOUNTAIN TREK, ANDORRA

You won't descend below 1500 metres (4921 feet) on this high-altitude, grade-eight mountain trek through cloud-tickling Andorra, one of the world's smallest countries, in the Pyrenees Mountains between France and Spain. Ramblers Walking Holidays' five-day itinerary follows a 97-kilometre (60-mile) circuit known as the Crown of Lakes. It threads its way through woodlands and alpine meadows and past lakes, waterfalls and snow-flecked slopes. You'll sleep in four comfortable (but remote and charmingly rustic) mountain refuges from which you'll eat hearty food and drink local wine before settling in to watch the sun set over stunning mountains peaking to the horizon. When the sun has said goodbye, the view is replaced with a velvety night sky scattered with stars. Other highlights include sunrises over the peak of Comapedrosa, views of the Incles Valley and chance sightings of a cute array of animals native to the area — wild boars, marmots (large squirrels), wood grouses, chamois (goat-antelopes), chevreuil (roe deer) and moufflons (wild sheep descendants). Expect to walk an average ten to 11 hours each day. The final 11-hour leg is a rough walk along the steep slopes of Els Aspres. It's the toughest day, but the rewards of accomplishment come soon after.

-O- ramblersholidays.co.uk/andorra-mountain-trek

The wooded valleys and undisturbed forests of America's oldest and most popular mountain range, the Appalachians, are the highlight of this 11-day walking and camping tour by Grand American Adventures. Geared to hikers and nature lovers, the itinerary plots a course through the many mountain ranges of Vermont, New Hampshire, Maine and Massachusetts, with a serious moderate to strenuous walk on the agenda each day. On day two, for example, the Mount Hunger Trail is a 6-kilometre (3.7-mile) steep climb rewarding you with impressive mountainous views of the New Hampshire Presidential Range. On day three you might spot moose and bear on the 18-kilometre (11-mile) Worcester Via Skyline trail, which has views of Vermont's most stunning ridges. On day five the 14-kilometre (9-mile) Franconia Ridge trail, one of the best in New England, scales three peaks: Little Haystack, Mount Lincoln and Mount Lafayette. The highlight for most is Baxter State Park, home to Mount Katahdin, the finishing point of the 3500-kilometre (2190-mile) Appalachian Trail, and one of the most remote wilderness areas in the eastern USA. It's a haven virtually untouched since the days of the first settlers. Time your run for autumn when the leaves are a riot of crimson and orange.

APPALACHIAN AND NEW ENGLAND WALK, USA

....

-O- grandamericanadventures.com/new-england-tours/
    walking/appalachian-trail-hiking

CAMINO DE SANTIAGO, SPAIN, PORTUGAL AND FRANCE

For centuries pilgrims from across Europe have walked the Camino de Santiago, a network of trails that culminate in the north-western Spanish city of Galicia at its cathedral of Santiago de Compostela (where, it's rumoured, lie the remains of an apostle). The popularity of the Camino has exploded in recent years, with 327,328 'certificates of completion' handed out in 2018 alone. But it's not necessarily for religious reasons. A survey by speciality operator CaminoWays reports that, while 28 per cent of walkers do it for religious or spiritual reasons, 17.8 per cent hit the trail to get away from their daily life and connect with nature, 28.2 per cent want a physical and mental challenge, 10.8 per cent have health and exercise reasons and 4.6 per cent want a cultural immersion. The most famous route is the Camino Frances, which offers a challenge going over the Pyrenees, but alternative routes include the Portuguese Coastal Camion, a reflective traverse through the wild Atlantic beauty and sandy beaches of Northern Portugal, and the Camino del Norte along the wonderful northern coast from Basque Country. With 27 different routes, you have plenty of options. CaminoWays designs bespoke itineraries that include hand-picked accommodation, daily luggage transfers, walking notes and maps in advance.

....

-O- caminoways.com/ways

BIBBULMUN WALK, ALBANY AND DENMARK, AUSTRALIA

Opened in 1998, the Bibbulmun Track is one of Australia's (if not the world's) great long-distance walking trails. It stretches nearly 1000 kilometres (620 miles) from Kalamunda near the Western Australian capital of Perth to the small town of Albany on the south coast, a journey that cuts through the heart of the scenic south-west corner of the country. The track boasts a variety of experiences from a sandy stroll to an eight-week trek, but the aim is the same – an on-foot, slow travel wilderness adventure. Do it by yourself navigating via purpose-built campsites (with timber shelters, water tanks and bush toilets) or sign up for Walk into Luxury's four-day Icons of Albany and Denmark trek, which canvasses a 43-kilometre section near this region. You'll follow the wild cliff-top coastline along pristine bays and empty windswept beaches and through three extraordinary national parks (Williams Bay, West Cape Howe and Torndirrup) where you can swim at Greens Pool, a turquoise oasis sheltered by large granite boulders (it's so calm and pristine the locals do laps here). Don't miss the viewing platform 40 metres (131 feet) above the Gap, a great rock chasm surging ferociously with Southern Ocean force. End the days in plush guesthouse accommodation with local gourmet food and wine.

....

-O- bibbulmuntrack.org.au
-O- walkintoluxury.com.au

WALKING MOROCCO'S UNDISCOVERED COAST, MOROCCO

Lose yourself on the wave-swept sandy beaches along the wild Atlantic coast of Morocco on this eight-day KE Adventures walking and cultural tour. Each day features a walk between two and six hours along dramatic cliffs, hidden footpaths and crusted sandy beaches. On the way you'll pass through the sleepy hamlets and whitewashed houses of Imessouane and the coastal fishing village of Tafedna with its beached fishing boats and Portuguese-influenced white-and-blue houses. Another walking highlight is the Argan forest, or Argania, where goats graze on the scrubby plants and Argan oil is produced by the local women's cooperatives. You'll camp on the beach one night and, on another, atop a cliff with Atlantic Ocean views direct from your tent. The penultimate night includes a stay in a characteristic old riad, in the heart of the 18th-century fortified medina of Essaouira. Here you can rest in the traditional inner courtyard before exploring the rest of the spice-scented World Heritage–listed old town. The journey starts and ends in Marrakech where exotic souks and colourful squares are the final evocative calling-card.

....

-O- keadventure.com/holidays/morocco-walking-marrakech-essaouira-berber-atlantic

You'll camp on the beach one night and, on another, atop a cliff with Atlantic Ocean views direct from your tent.

JURA CREST TRAIL, SWITZERLAND

The oldest long-distance trail in Switzerland is a bit of a local secret that is well-loved for its combination of moderately graded walking, panoramic alpine scenery and relatively tourist-free remoteness. It connects the two Swiss cities of Zurich and Geneva over the Jura mountains along a big north-westerly arc with panoramas of the Swiss Central Plateau, the Alps, the Mittelland Lakes and the Bernese Oberland. The trail is 320 kilometres (199 miles) and you can cover 93 kilometres (58 miles) of that on Tourradar's eight-day self-guided walk. It begins in the German-speaking Canton of Solothurn and ends in the French-speaking canton of Neuchatel and the town of Couvet, so you'll cross through two language regions (and distinct architectural styles) on the way. By day you'll trek along high ridge-lines, past sparkling lakes and through meadows and forests. On day five you'll walk through Chaux-de-Fonds, a town with a centuries-old watchmaking heritage. On day seven you'll get up close to the natural rock amphitheatre of Creux du Van, the Swiss equivalent of the Grand Canyon. In the evenings, you drop down into the little market towns to stay in authentic Swiss inns that serve local dishes such as toétché, a savoury cream cake, and Jura's own Bellelay cheese.

....

-O- *tourradar.com/t/105538*

BANFF HIKE ADVENTURE, ALBERTA, CANADA

Banff National Park in the Canadian Rocky Mountains is a World Heritage site and Canada's oldest national park – Canucks have been singing its praises since 1885. This six-day Austin Adventures hiking expedition puts the sure-footed among us on top of the world; it's an eye-popping trek past white-tipped jagged mountains, glistening waterfalls and turquoise glacial lakes (Chateau Lake Louise being a highlight). Look out for local residents such as grizzly bears, elk and bighorn sheep, while an expert guide shares the low-down on this unique ecosystem above the tree-line. There's a full-day hike over famed Sentinel Pass to look forward to, plus a day hiking the Athabasca glacier with crampons strapped on. You'll also float into the clouds on a gondola-lift ride to the beautiful wildflower-strewn alpine oasis known as Sunshine Meadows. Enjoy hours on end of natural-world isolation before retreating each night to cosy lodge accommodation, the kind with open fires, wood furnishings and Canadian craftwork. The trip starts and ends in Calgary.

···

-O- austinadventures.com/packages/alberta-banff-hike

Overleaf: Pristine mountain lakes on the Banff hike in Canada

THE ROMAN ROAD TO THE MONASTERY OF SANTA MARIA, PORTUGAL

Tucked away in the north-western corner of Portugal amid vine-lined hills and iridescent green valleys, rural communities still practise centuries-old customs and rituals. The region's old paved tracks and footpaths are the ideal terrain for walkers to engage with the locals in rustic old villages and surrounding fields (where farmers keep long-horned cattle in distinctive granite espigueiros). This seven-night self-guided trip, beginning in Soajo and ending in Santa Maria do Bouro, is an easy to moderate zig-zag walk southward. You can bite off between 11 and 23 kilometres (7–14 miles) per day (3–6.5 hours) or take the shorter 8–17-kilometre (5–11-mile) options (2–4 hours, using lifts) depending on energy levels. Along the way there's a feast of charming scenery including the well-preserved lakeside Castle of Lindoso, the wild Serra Amarela and spectacular Ribeira de Carcerelha, and a Roman bridge over the Rio Homem and the pass at Alto Moraço. From Braga to Astorga you'll traverse the old Roman road as it contours around the hillside, gently descending towards Chorense and Emaús with Roman mileposts along the way. The food promises to be hearty and wholesome including caldo verde soup, the ubiquitous bacalhau and beef from the barrosã cow. The journey ends as the name suggests at the monastery, now the Pousada Santa Maria do Bouro, where you can indulge in a well-earned swim in the pool.

···

-O- onfootholidays.co.uk/routes/northern-portugal

GO BEYOND

Slow pursuits in far-flung places

The faint-hearted need not apply. Those wanting to live on the edge or get lost in transformation often achieve their quest by pushing their minds, bodies and boundaries to the outer limits where there is no such thing as a comfort zone. Choosing to do it away from the built-up environment in extreme locations provides the added bonus of a digital detox, an off-grid experience, an immersion with locals and a place in the wild, natural world where few have gone before. The concept of danger comes into play here too. While your heart might be beating at a million miles a minute, rest assured your mind will need to be ever-present. Call it adrenaline-induced mindfulness. I'd love to tell you about one of my 'slow to the extreme' experiences, but I admit to having a gap on my travel résumé – I'd rather travel with David Attenborough than Bear Grylls. There's no shame in that, surely. You latter travel types go enjoy the extremities of the planet (just make sure you come home to tell us all about it).

Top: Pinnacles in Gunung Mulu National Park on the Lost Explorer itinerary, Borneo

Right top: Desert dunes on one of the Get Lost itineraries

Right bottom: The Nenets Reindeer Migration trip in Russia's Arctic Circle

ABSEIL 'THE LOST WORLD', VENEZUELA

Extreme isolation is one of the challenges facing punters on the Secret Compass Venezuelan abseiling itinerary – but just imagine the view! This annual expedition into a region made famous by Arthur Conan Doyle's novel *The Lost World* begins with a trek through the World Heritage–listed Canaima National Park. You'll take the reverse route charted in 1937 by American aviator and adventurer Jimmie Angel, who was forced to find his way out of the jungle after crash-landing on a mountain. Known as Auyán-tepui, it's an imposing tabletop mountain home to Angel Falls, the world's highest waterfalls. Once you've made it to the summit, it's time to step into oblivion, as they say, by abseiling down this incredible 979-metre-high (3212-foot-high) natural phenomenon. The descent, with yawning otherworldly jungle-green views and not a soul in sight, takes two days, including a night's camping halfway down the length of the falls. If there was ever a time to use the word epic, it's here. Epic.

-O- secretcompass.com/expedition/venezuela-abseil-angel-falls-expedition

GETTING LOST, GLOBAL

Sometimes you need to lose yourself in order to find yourself and Black Tomato has figured out a means in a GPS-riddled world to help you along that road. The Get Lost series of adventures have their ground zero in uncharted destinations, be they polar, jungle, desert, mountain or coastal environments. If you're looking to layer a challenge on top of a challenge on top of a challenge, you can sign up for a trip without knowing where you're going or what you'll need (apart from inner steel). You can choose the environment you want (but not the country), or – the ultimate test – let Black Tomato choose it for you. Either way, you won't know where you're going until you get there. Once in-situ it's up to you, the modern-world explorer, to use wits and skill to navigate the way back. You'll have a realistic sense of being lost, but with the help of pre-trip training and the right kit and equipment you'll be equipped to get yourself to mapped-out check-in points. And before you go thinking this is the most barmy idea on the planet, take solace in the fact that an experienced expedition ops team will track your progress. You just won't be able to see them.

-O- blacktomato.com/get-lost

Top: Walking out of the Venezuelan jungle

Bottom: A reflective moment on a Get Lost adventure

UNION GLACIERS CAMP, ANTARCTICA

Modern-day adventurers are still following in the footsteps of 18th-century Antarctic explorers, taking on incredible experiences in the face of extreme landscapes that only the lucky few will ever encounter. Union Glacier Camp, run by Antarctic Logistics and Expeditions (ALE), is a camp-out for travellers mettle-testing Antarctica's spectacular and remote Ellsworth Mountains, which lie 2991 kilometres (1859 miles) from the southern tip of Chile and a short flight from Mount Vinson, the highest peak in Antarctica. It's only accessible by air, so travellers will touch down on the naturally occurring blue-ice runway atop Union Glacier. The main camp pops-up for Antarctic summer (November–January) housing up to 70 guests in dual-occupancy clam tents (double-walled Antarctic-strength sleeping tents with a high-tech nylon covering and durable aluminium frame that opens up like a clam shell). Visitors can upsize to the exclusive Three Glaciers Camp, a retreat limited to just eight sleeping suites with a maximum occupancy of 16 guests. All tents are heated and equipped with power for charging personal electronics and there's a dedicated private chef. Guests at both camps (be they skiers, climbers or snowmobilers) can immerse in a frigid terrain of glaciers and frozen sea. Venture to the summit of Mount Vinson, journey to an emperor penguin colony, attempt an expedition in the spirit of early explorers or, and this is the holy grail, head to the South Pole for an overnight camp. You'll wake up at the latitude of 90 degrees south with all 360 lines of longitude meeting at your feet. In just a few steps you can walk around the world. Not that you'll be short on things to boast about.

....

-O- antarctic-logistics.com/services/camp-services

REINDEER MIGRATION WITH THE NENETS, ARCTIC CIRCLE, RUSSIA

Siberia's Yamal Peninsula, in the Arctic Circle, roughly 2000 kilometres (1240 miles) north-east of Moscow, is the home of the self-reliant Nenets, the indigenous nomads who eke out a life in one of the most extreme environments on Earth. Temperatures here frequently drop below – repeat, below – both minus 40 degrees Celsius and Fahrenheit. Brave and curious travellers will step into this frozen land 'at the edge of human endurance' to join Secret Compass on the Nenets' annual reindeer migration across the Arctic tundra. The tours are timed with one of two yearly festivals that sees the Nenets migrating their 3500-strong herd of reindeer 60 kilometres (37 miles) across the frozen Gulf of Ob, on the Arctic Ocean. The 24-hour migration, with the team keeping pace in all-terrain vehicles and sledges, is a race against time. With no pasture along the route, the Nenets must get the reindeer across the gulf before they become hungry and weak. Word of warning from the tour company: 'There will be no breaks for the herders, the vehicles, the animals or for you.' The crossing, which culminates in the annual Reindeer Herding Festival in Yar Sale, is a highlight of the expedition. It's up there with the immersive opportunity of connecting with nomadic life. You'll stay with Nenet hosts, wear traditional herder coats and boots, help with chores, eat what they eat (such as reindeer stews and risotto-like rice dishes) and sleep in their tepee-style reindeer-hide tents called chums (pronounced 'chooms'). Freezing, unforgiving and completely unforgettable.

-O- secretcompass.com/expedition/nenets-reindeer-migration-arctic-expedition

BECOME A LOST EXPLORER IN BORNEO, MALAYSIA

It's increasingly difficult to follow the road less travelled, but the boundary-pushing peeps at Black Tomato seem to find a way. The 12-night Lost Explorer itinerary is a mind, body and spirit cleanse in the Sarawak Jungle of Borneo, where survival depends on learning 'to thrive like the nomadic Penan jungle tribe', one of the world's last remaining nomadic jungle tribes. You'll take a dug-out canoe to the home of the Penan, who, over the following days, will give you a masterclass on jungle survival. You'll learn about edible plants, lay traps to catch wild pigs, fish, build your own campfires and off-the-ground shelters, identify tracks of animals such as the sun bear, recognise bird calls and sleep in the wilderness in a hammock. Some of the more intriguing lessons include making a blow-pipe dart and learning forest sign-language using cut twigs and folded leaves, both vital for hunting. If all that sounds challenging enough, think again. Next, you'll be taken to a jungle waterfall where you'll set up camp for the night. While a Penan guide will always be within howling distance for emergencies, you'll ostensibly be left alone in the jungle to fend for yourself for a whole 48 hours. Good luck!

....

-O- blacktomato.com/destinations/borneo/lost-explorer-borneo

LUT DESERT STARS AND SOLITUDE EXPEDITION, IRAN

Also known as the Dasht-e-Lut, Iran's Lut desert is a photogenic landscape of stark shadows, shifting sands and towering kaluts – the dramatic flat-topped mesas that rise from the sand like castles. Covering a region of some 51,800 square kilometres (20,000 square miles), it is also home to the hottest recorded place on Earth. Through this extreme environment (temperatures during November when the expedition takes place can still reach up to 35 degrees Celsius, or 95 degrees Fahrenheit), Secret Compass leads the more adventurous among us on a 13-day 220-kilometre (137-mile) east–west expedition, traversing dunes, kaluts and meteorite fields. This boundary-pushing venture, following in the footsteps of explorers Marco Polo (1271) and William Thesiger (1964) and very few others, is completed almost entirely on foot, with participants each carrying daypacks with clothing layers, water (at least three litres per person), lunch and a few essentials. Support and extra water is supplied by four-wheel-drive vehicles, which make themselves scarce during the day. You camp in tents by night underneath the starry black sky and won't shower for days on end. Other highlights of this rare experience include passing through former Silk Road haunts and seeing Kerman, one of Iran's oldest cities.

....

-O- secretcompass.com/expedition/iran-lut-desert-expedition

GETTING AWAY

When camping in Antarctica is not an option but you seek peace and quiet in remote and lofty places, these rather more comfortable getaways might require some journeying to, but the effort will reward on arrival.

ADLER MOUNTAIN LODGE, ITALY

The alpine village of Alpe Di Siusi, in the heart of the Italian Dolomites, is home to the Adler Mountain Lodge (not to mention some of the purest, clearest air on the planet). Its locale, in a World Heritage site recognised for its outstanding natural beauty, ensured it took ten years to plan and build, but the rewards speak for themselves. A central wooden lodge is the dining, lounge and wellness hub for 30 rooms including 12 small chalets made entirely of local spruce wood and modelled on old Tyrolean mountain huts. Guests have wildflowers and walks in summer, ski slopes in winter and spa sessions year-round.

-O- adler-lodge.com/en/hotel-alpe-di-siusi/1-0.html

SAL SALIS, AUSTRALIA

On the stunningly remote west coast of Australia, Ningaloo Reef, extending 260 kilometres (162 miles), is one of the world's most memorably wild and pristine environments. You can join eco-tourist operators to swim alongside whale sharks and humpback whales in the turquoise waters, see turtle hatchlings digging their way out of the sand, and snorkel straight from the beach over colourful corals and hundreds of different sea creatures. Running alongside the reef is Cape Range National Park, an equally impressive limestone escarpment that is home to Sal Salis, a luxury resort with 16 safari tents artfully camouflaged against the dunes and native scrub. There's no wifi, and guests are limited to solar power, composting toilets and 20 litres of water per day, but these factors add to that rarefied feeling of being miles from anywhere.

-O- salsalis.com.au

SHELDON CHALET, ALASKA

Anchored deep into the granite nunatak (a glacier island) on the flanks of North America's highest mountain, Mount Denali (6190 metres; 20,310 feet), this luxury mountaineer's paradise – with flight-only access – is an engineering marvel. Its hexagonal structure ensures each of the five guest rooms features views across the jagged mountains of the Alaska Range or along the sloping Don Sheldon amphitheatre carved over millennia by the ice of Ruth Glacier. At night, an aurora borealis and shooting star lightshow can be viewed from the firelit dining room or from under the covers through expansive windows. To say this is a bucket-list experience is to seriously understate it – if you only have one more luxury slow trip of a lifetime, this is up there with the best.

-O- sheldonchalet.com

Left: A local on the Nenets Reindeer Migration in Russia's Arctic Circle (see p. 76)

Top: Stunning views from the Adler Mountain Lodge in the Dolomites, Italy

ARISTI MOUNTAIN RESORT AND VILLAS, GREECE

Built from stone and wood, the luxury rooms and villas at this resort in north-western Greece fit with the surrounding traditional village of Aristi, in west Zagori. Being a four-hour drive to the nearest airport in Thessaloniki, Zagori is hardly on the tourist radar, but its status as a World Heritage contender is a nod to the surrounding aged landscape replete with old arched stone bridges, cobbled streets, picturesque village squares, incredible gorges and alpine lakes.

-O- aristi.eu/en

BERKELEY RIVER LODGE, AUSTRALIA

This extraordinary high-end lodge has been built, somewhat miraculously, in one of the most remote places on Earth, the Kimberley Coast. When you're here at the top-end of Western Australia, the next stop is Timor Leste, in Asia. Accessible only by air via Darwin, getting to this wilderness area is part of the adventure – the red-dirt airstrip might as well be another planet. Strung along the coastal dunes, fourteen villas overlook the white sands and blue Timor Sea. Guests can explore the Berkeley River by boat, the beach by four-wheel drive and the King George River by chopper, or just keep tabs on the natural world from the comfort of verandah recliners and an outdoor bath.

-O- berkeleyriverlodge.com.au

Top: Picturesque Aristi, Greece

Right: Western Australia's King George River, part of the Berkeley River Lodge experience

Overleaf: Up close on the Nenets Reindeer Migration in Russia's Arctic Circle (see p. 76)

THE BROADMOOR, USA

A trio of remote wilderness properties at the Broadmoor resort in Colorado Springs are serviced by a fleet of Cadillacs, but one of the wilderness properties can also be reached by foot (on a rewarding three-hour trek) or by mule. Cloud Camp is a seven-room wood-and-stone lodge (an additional 11 cabins are nearby) that sits atop Cheyenne Mountain with 360-degree views taking in the plains, Pikes Peak and the Colorado Rocky Mountains. The mules, which come from the Grand Canyon, are huggable sherpas and make for a memorable, Instagrammable arrival. Rest assured, your luggage is transferred via Cadillac.

-O- broadmoor.com/cloud-camp

SHAKTI 360 LETI, INDIA

India's Kumaon Himalayas is a little-known region of Uttarakhand; residents of its mountain villages still live traditional lives. Amid the wildflowers and terraced slopes sits beautiful Shakti 360 Leti, a modern property that blends into the wooded surrounds. Far removed from the noise and chaos, this remote mountain-top location has views of the perennially snow-capped peaks of the Great Himalaya range. You can trek through the pretty foothill terrain to one of the four luxuriously lofty lodges or take the next step and join one of the property's multi-day village walks.

-O- shaktihimalaya.com/kumaon.php

STAYING AFLOAT

Boat journeys

When I was 16, on the verge of finishing year 11 at school, I had the opportunity and enough of an adventurous spirit to go on a week-long tall ship voyage on Australia's *Young Endeavour*, an experience designed to build resilience and confidence in teenagers. Part of that meant working four-hour shifts through the night alongside the crew. On one such shift beginning at midnight, all bleary-eyed and tired, I climbed into the sail box for some quick shut-eye only to wake an hour later with the skipper in emergency mode, thinking I'd gone overboard. I was henceforth relegated to the galley where, slowly, with time, I won back respect by cooking some top-notch food.

Top: L'Impressionniste *travels through the French countryside*

Right top: Steam Ship Sudan *cruises Egypt's Nile*

Right bottom: Indonesia's Raja Ampat Islands on the Bird's Head Seascape journey

... the tiptoe of a paddle dipping into a skin of water, the tinkering of sails against a mast, the lapping of water against hull.

That was my first boating adventure and, despite a rather awkward start, I've been on many since. From the adventurous – a canoe-camping journey down Australia's Katherine River, a felucca trip down Egypt's Nile River, a rice-barge cruise down the Mekong in Laos – to the more elaborate – a barge journey in rural France and a small-vessel cruise through the dazzlingly remote Kimberley in Western Australia. Though they're in diverse locations, on vastly different vessels, and powered variously by paddle, wind and diesel, the experiences share similarities that tap into slow travel. Water is obviously at the heart of it. A floating itinerary takes you along a route you would be unlikely to journey on otherwise. Rivers, tributaries and oceans create different pathways that expose the traveller to exotic scenery, native creatures, different smells and sounds – the tiptoe of a paddle dipping into a skin of water, the tinkering of sails against a mast, the lapping of water against hull. Like train trips, you can sit back on a boat and let the captain, the current or the wind carry you forward.

L'IMPRESSIONNISTE BARGE CRUISE, FRANCE

The achingly enchanting *L'Impressionniste*, painted in red, blue and black with the French flag flying at its stern, is a 12-passenger wooden barge. It's named for the 19th-century art period, which is alluringly reminiscent of the French countryside on Outdoor Travel's seven-day itinerary from Fleurey-sur-Ouche to Escommes through the Ouche Valley in Southern Burgundy. The cabins, which each bear the names of renowned Impressionist painters, are comfortable (double beds and ensuites) and fittingly charming with picture windows and wall-prints. Teak flooring, balloon-backed dining chairs and leather sofas make the saloon similarly hospitable. From the barge's geranium-scented wooden deck, the distinctive French scenery rolls out: charming lockhouses and vine-striped fields to medieval villages and fortified hilltops that can be seen as you putt-putt around the bend in the river. Burgundy is famed for its history and viticulture and the stops are intrinsically linked to these themes. You'll walk the markets and mustard shops of Dijon, indulge in a wine-tasting in the wine capital of Beaune and visit the moat-encircled Château de Commarin for a private falconry demonstration. You can also disembark to walk or cycle along the ever-present towpath.

-O- *outdoortravel.com.au*

SOUTHERN QUEST, AUSTRALIA

Three decks high and cutting a fine figure against enormous red cliffs, the nine-cabin *Kimberley Quest II* is a luxury vessel custom-built for exploring Western Australia's wild and unfathomably remote Kimberley wilderness region. Kimberley Quest's Southern Quest itinerary (a bucket-lister I was lucky enough to tick off in 2018) begins with a small plane ride from the pearling town of Broome to the palm-spiked Mitchell Plateau, from where it's a chopper ride to the boat berthed in the middle of the Hunter River. The eight-day journey back to Broome is Attenborough-esque in its appeal. Aided by a jetboat and three smaller tenders, the days are spent exploring beaches, fishing and birdwatching (with croc-spotting thrown in). Enjoy walks to freshwater swimming holes and hikes to the Indigenous rock-art caves. When the boat ups anchor, the sundeck is the spot for whale-watching, taking in the passing landscapes or stargazing. There's also a small library for natural-world fans. Memorable highlights include cooking fresh-plucked rock oysters in the embers of a beach fire and witnessing the receding tide at Montgomery Reef, a natural phenomenon where remote coral-capped limestone appears to miraculously rise from the water as the tide goes down.

-O- *kimberleyquest.com.au/kimberley-cruises/8-day-southern-kimberley-cruise.php*

FRANZ JOSEF LAND EXPLORER, RUSSIA

The *Greg Mortimer*, a new advanced expedition vessel built to world-class polar standards, will be your comfortable home base on Aurora Expeditions' 16-day Franz Josef Land Explorer tour. The voyage, with expert photographers on board, sets off from Kirkenes, Norway, bunny-hops to Murmansk, Russia, then crosses the Barents Sea to complete a circle of Franz Josef Land. Covering an area of 16,134 square kilometres (6229 square miles), this icy Arctic Ocean archipelago is a starkly beautiful glaciated world with 191 islands inhabited by incredible wildlife. Millions of seabirds nest on the archipelago every year (the Brünnich's guillemot, purple sandpiper, Arctic skua, ivory gull and Arctic tern among them), but the real highlight is seeing polar bears and walruses against the icy backdrop. The vessel has a unique hydraulic viewing platform that folds out for unobstructed views of passing marine life including humpback, narwhal, white beluga and the elusive bowhead whales. It also has special zodiac platforms for easy island landings where you can photograph unique stone spheres on Cham Island and visit fascinating historic explorer huts. There's also an activity platform for launching sea kayaks so you can paddle among the ice floes.

....

-O- *auroraexpeditions.com.au/expedition/franz-josef-land-explorer*

You'll pass by Malabar's palm-fronded banks, where children play and grandparents fish.

LOTUS HOUSEBOAT, INDIA

The rattan-topped *Lotus* houseboat is a gorgeously traditional rice barge that has been heart-warmingly converted into a floating guesthouse. Its watery wonderland is the beautiful and serene backwater of Malabar, a region bounded by the Arabian Sea on India's south-western shores in Northern Kerala. If you can snaffle one of only two cabins, named 'Sukhima' (Happiness) and 'Lalima' (Beauty), you'll enjoy bedrooms with teak floors, ethnic furniture, temple-style murals and colourful throw-cushions, plus the home comforts of an ensuite with bath and shower, ceiling fans, large windows and balconies with rattan chairs. When you're not in your room, make use of the teak recliners on the rooftop sundeck. The itinerary takes travellers across the tea and coffee plantations of Coorg Hills to Valiyaparamba village and Monkey Island then onwards to the Sultan Canal. You'll pass by Malabar's palm-fronded banks, where children play and grandparents fish. Stops include Snake Temple, dedicated to Goddess Badrakali, Shiva Temple at Payyannur and, on the final night, Shri Mutthappan Temple and its famous evening ceremony. Little extras include low-impact canoe tours in the smaller canals and sustainable fishing with the opportunity to cook your catch. On shore, you can explore by bike and take your time meandering around the waterways.

....

-O- *secret-retreats.com/en/discover/india/kerala/lotus-houseboat*

KATHERINE RIVER CANOEING, AUSTRALIA

Tourists up in the Top End town of Katherine in Australia's Northern Territory tend to board boats for trips to the famed Katherine Gorge, which lies 32 kilometres (20 miles) out of town. Slow travellers can sidestep the tourist mayhem by heading in the opposite direction to a quieter stretch of the Katherine River that makes for perfect kayaking country. The Katherine River springs in Nitmiluk National Park and carves its way through 13 gorges in the Arnhem Land Plateau. It is the main artery through the town of Katherine, an isolated community of about 6000 people, 320 kilometres (199 miles) south of Darwin. A while back I joined Gecko Canoeing and Trekking for a three-day, 40-kilometre (25-mile) downstream paddle through this river country. Often described as 'where the tropics meet the outback', the region is a raw, ancient and serene place to dip the paddle in. You put clothes and provided swags, tents, sleeping bags and a campfire chair into the canoe holds, and the guide brings the rest, including the food. The alternating rapids and waterholes, which figure in the creation story of the Indigenous Wardaman people, reveal schools of barramundi and freshwater stingray skimming below the surface. The sandy banks are habitat to spectacular birds, agile wallabies that bound off into the scrub, and other wildlife including a (very small) croc or two. Tents are pitched in the sand for a peaceful riverside sleep.

....

-O- geckocanoeing.com.au/project/3-day-katherine-river-hiatus

STEAM SHIP SUDAN, EGYPT

The date palms, the flat-roofed desert villas, the felucca sails – a boat trip down Egypt's Nile is a dreamily slow eye on a landscape that has hardly changed in centuries. Taking it all in, the Steam Ship *Sudan* is an authentic 19th-century steamer that plies the waters of the Nile between Luxor and Aswan. The ship itself, once the writing retreat for murder-mystery author Agatha Christie, evokes the romance and nostalgia of the heyday of luxury travel. Its two decks of cabins are adorned in the Belle Époque style with beautiful wood-panelling, brass beds and colourful African ornaments. The 1930s dining room is like a movie set, with crisp white tablecloths, grand candelabras, opulent dishes and waistcoated staff. Original Travel's three- and four-night itineraries (part of a ten-day Taste of the Nile trip) include embarkations at many of Egypt's most popular attractions, such as Valley of the Kings, the limestone valley with burial chambers of the great pharaohs including Tutankhamen; the Temple of Edfu, one of the best preserved temples in Egypt built in honour of the falcon-headed sky god, Horus; and the Temple of Philae, one of the most important shrines in ancient Egypt until 550CE.

....

-O- originaltravel.co.uk/itineraries/a-taste-of-the-nile

It looks vintage, but this 26-metre (85-foot) handcrafted wooded yacht was actually constructed in 2017. Named after the giant Sequoia tree, one of the oldest living organisms on Earth, it was built using traditional Indonesian Bugis boat techniques, making use of ironwood and teak and adopting the traditional Sulawesi hull construction (named a UNESCO Intangible Cultural Heritage of Humanity). Almost every detail on board *Sequoia* has been handcrafted by local artisans, including the three suites with wood-panelled walls, teak furnishings, ironwood floors, a woven rattan king bed and fittings such as a curved staircase and carved wood architraves. Giving ballast to the old is a state-of-the-art American engine, electrical systems, a spacious guestroom, a rooftop deck and a gourmet kitchen. Secret Retreats' Bird's Head Seascape itinerary is an 11-day journey from Raja Ampat to Triton Bay, a relatively untouched archipelago off the Bird's Head Peninsula, West Papua. With a cruising distance of 925 kilometres (575 miles) you'll swim, scuba dive, kayak and snorkel in the world's most biodiverse marine ecosystem, which boasts 12 marine protected areas teeming with reef fish, coral, whales, turtles, dugongs and saltwater crocodiles. Team this with beach picnics, rooftop cocktails and cuisine cooked by local hosts for a perfect slow travel escape.

BIRD'S HEAD SEASCAPE, INDONESIA

....

-O- secret-retreats.com/en/discover/indonesia/raja-
    ampat/sequoia-yacht

THE SOUTH PACIFIC SEA OF DREAMS, VANUATU

The traditional sailing vessels of the Pacific Island nations are known as Vaka Moanas. These double-hulled sailing boats are, like catamarans, joined in the middle with a deck that supports two acute-angled and ancient-looking triangle sails. Designed to skim over the reefs and shallow waters with wind power, and to navigate by the stars, the vessels are still one of the quickest ways to island-hop in Vanuatu. Blue Flowers' 15-day Sea of Dreams itinerary in the South Pacific includes a three-day sailing trip on one of these historic vessels. With room enough on board to sleep eight people, the vessel sets sail from Port Vila where you'll be welcomed on board by expert sailors who keep alive the stories and customs of their people. You'll sail under the night sky on an endless ocean with just the stars and the sound of the waves for company. At dawn, you wake as the Vaka approaches a hidden cove on the island of Tanna, where the crew serves freshly caught fish, cooked on an open fire. As the breeze picks up, you journey to another beach and a waterfall, before the return journey to Port Vila. With the wind, sand and salt in your hair, you'll feel both physically and mentally absorbed in this paradisiacal place.

-O- *blueflower.la/destination/oceania/vanuatu/vanuatu-new-caledonia-travel.html*

AN ISLAND HOME

When you think of boats, the mind tends to drift on the waves to islands; similarly, when you think of islands, the mind conjures boats. There's something about the serenity of being surrounded by sea and the sensation of being remote that makes us feel like tiny specks in an infinite universe. Get yourself to an island some time soon.

TORY ISLAND, IRELAND

Tory Island – or Toraigh in Irish – is a wild, treeless tabletop of an island 14.5 kilometres (9 miles) off the coast of County Donegal in Ulster. It's only accessible by passenger ferry and, being cut off from the mainland, has established itself as a destination steeped in history, mythology and folklore. It has its own brand of monarchy – a strongly held tradition that sees the resident 144 or so local Gaeltacht villagers choosing their own king (basically a spokesperson for the island) – and a quirky community of artists who run the art gallery. But the main attraction is the treeless, wind-ruffled and cliff-skirted landscape and its intriguing remnant Irish history. Dún Bhaloir (Balor's Fort) has 90-metre-high (295-foot-high) cliffs on three sides and is accessible via a narrow isthmus. The 12th-century Tau Cross, carved from a single slab of slate, is one of only two left in Ireland.

-O- wildatlanticway.com/home

FOGO ISLAND, CANADA

Off the unforgiving coastline of Newfoundland, Canada, remote Fogo Island, once the centre of cod fishing, is now known for its subarctic wilderness. Trails and ancient footpaths weave past jagged cliffs and through aged pine forests where herds of caribou gather. Beyond the shores, icebergs float in the North Atlantic waters, puffins bob on the waves and whales make a show of breaching. Cultural tastemakers have also deemed this a destination for minimalist architecture enthusiasts. The island's holy grail is the Fogo Island Inn, an astonishing building perched on stilts along a desolate coastline. Its radical design, like a cubist ship moored to the bedrock, includes 29 rooms with floor-to-ceiling views, a contemporary art gallery, a heritage library, rooftop saunas and a two-day 'Architecture at the Edge' itinerary.

-O- fogoislandinn.ca

ALPHONSE ISLAND, SEYCHELLES

Think of an island paradise and the image that comes to mind will likely look something like Alphonse Island, one of three on an atoll in the Indian Ocean, 250 kilometres (155 miles) from Mahé in the Seychelles. This unapologetically off-grid Eden has unblemished white-as-salt shorelines, sea-flats where the shadows of fish flit across the sand and protected coral reefs alive with colours. The island's only resort has suites, bungalows and thatched-roof villas tucked into the tropical gardens just back from the beach. There's conventional resort entertainment (a tennis court and swimming pool), but the ocean beckons – snorkel, swim and scuba dive for a chance to see resident spinner dolphins, manta rays and giant tortoises. You can also take part in conservation incentives including planting an endemic tree.

-O- alphonse-island.com/en

Left: Wildlife on Alphonse Island
Right: The architecturally striking Fogo Island Inn

DIRK HARTOG ISLAND, AUSTRALIA

Known in Western Australia as an 'ark' for its endangered wildlife, this remote island lies in the mesmeric Shark Bay World Heritage Area, the state's first World Heritage–listed site. It's accessible via plane, speedboat or vehicle ferry, and you might want to stay a while. There are camping sites in the coastal dunes of the national park and an Eco Lodge that sits 30 metres (just under 100 feet) from the jade-green water. Use it as a base to kayak and stand-up paddle board, and revel in the night-time fires, sunset drinks and fresh-caught fish barbecues. Loggerhead turtles, lemon sharks, white-breasted sea eagles and stingrays are among the wildlife to look out for in between visiting the island's blowholes, breathtaking rose-pink lake and seemingly endless beaches.

....

-O- dirkhartogisland.com

BIRD ISLAND, BELIZE

The words 'magical', 'must-do', 'peaceful' and 'beautiful' are oft-repeated in the reviews left by Airbnb guests staying on Bird Island. This private island, which can be booked for four to six guests exclusively (and has been promoted as one of Airbnb's best stays), is on an atoll 10 kilometres (6 miles) from Placencia village in Belize. It has three colourful adjoining weatherboard huts that are tricked up with holiday essentials – recliners, hammocks and an overwater cabana. There's an observatory overlooking the atoll and an enclosed swimming area with a gazebo. It's Robinson Crusoe style in that there's not another soul in sight. Snorkel among stingrays, barracuda, schools of feeding fish and diving pelicans or go for a kayak. Or just laze about and enjoy your own private island.

....

-O- birdislandplacencia.com

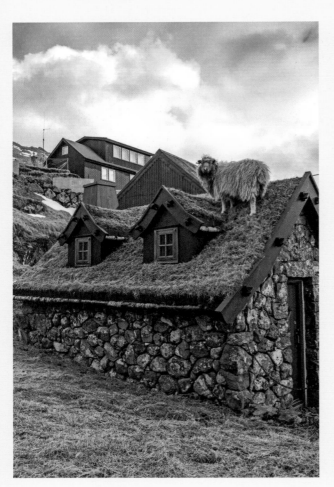

FAROE ISLANDS, DENMARK

Most people would struggle to locate the Faroe Islands on a map, but that's a huge part of its off-the-beaten-track allure. In the North Atlantic, 320 kilometres (199 miles) north-west of Scotland and about halfway between Norway and Iceland, this T-shaped archipelago is made up of 18 volcanic islands and hundreds of smaller ones, mostly connected by bridges, tunnels and roads. Though part of Denmark, the population of 49,000 is self-governing with its own parliament, language and sporting teams. Torshavn, the capital, has a fishing harbour and pretty red terrace houses, but you'll likely head into the rugged coastal countryside to point your binoculars at waterfalls that tumble into the ocean, gravity-defying sea stacks, a lighthouse teetering on a cliff ridge and sweet little villages with turf-roofed houses.

....

-O- visitfaroeislands.com

Left: Turf-roofed house (and guest), Faroe Islands

Right: The idyllic private island of Song Saa, Cambodia

Overleaf: Faroe Island's stunning scenery includes the Leitisvatn Cliffs

SIARGAO, PHILIPPINES

In the Philippines' province of Surigao del Norte, 800 kilometres (almost 500 miles) north of Manila, the island of Siargao is the kind of laidback place you once found in Thailand and Bali. The tiny teardrop-shaped island has 27 kilometres (17 miles) of peripheral white sands, reefs and waters that have the blue Pantone chart covered. You can get around the island's dirt roads in quirky jeepney vehicles or on motorbikes, and island-hopping is via traditional outrigger canoes. The renowned Cloud 9 surf spot, near the pier in the main town of General Luna, has some of the world's most kick-arse waves and is something of a pilgrimage destination for surfers. It's the kind of place you'll plan to visit for a week and end up staying for months.

....

-O- *tourism.gov.ph*

SONG SAÀ, CAMBODIA

The soft lull of waves, lantern-lit trails, candles floating in an infinity pool, a sea alive with bioluminescence – these are my memories of Song Saa, a private island resort about 40 minutes by speedboat from the Cambodian mainland. The resort is made up of two tiny islands joined by a wooden footbridge. Koh Bong is the resort's own national park and Koh Ouen is home to 27 thatched-roof jungle, sea-view and over-water villas. Both islands have an organic (rather than intentional) tropical-oasis ambience with driftwood fences, tropical flowers, palms and pandanus trees. The over-water restaurant, resembling an old fishing pier, has double-bed hammocks and offers a degustation menu featuring Khmer produce. You can don goggles to explore the marine park that extends 200 metres (656 feet) around both islands and visit Prek Svay village on nearby Koh Rong; these are two of Song Saa's many sustainable initiatives to restore and improve the local natural and human environment.

....

-O- *songsaa.com*

BOLTHOLES

Cabins, huts and shacks

In the dictionary a bolthole is described variously thus: 'a refuge, an escape'; 'a place where a person can escape and hide'; and, my favourite, 'somewhere you can go to get away from people you know'. So, you get the picture, right? The main thing to note is that boltholes come in all shapes and sizes, designs and landscapes, from cabins and huts to beach shacks and treehouses. Recent travel trends have also put glamping tents, pods and tiny houses on the map, tapping into the need for folks of all walks of life to escape the city, the shirt and the shite. Key, of course, to finding a bolthole is keeping it to yourself. Often, that's not easy. There's always someone sniffing around when you're trying to make a timely escape.

Top: Thermal water at Dunton Hot Springs Log Cabins in Colorado, USA

Right top: Glen Dye Cabins in the wilds of Scotland

Right bottom: South Devon's Beach Hut, England, has its own beach

GLEN DYE CABINS AND COTTAGES, ABERDEEN, SCOTLAND

Dubbed 'a restorative nature destination' by owners Caroline and Charlie Gladstone, Glen Dye Cabins and Cottages is nestled deep in the woodlands of Kincardineshire, a 40-minute drive from Aberdeen, Scotland. The property has a handful of converted cottages and a redesigned Victorian-era summer house, but the real drawcards are the immersive wilderness cabins including a fully renovated 1840s sawmill and a remodelled 1950s Airstream Safari Caravan, both of which sit under fairy lights in a shadowy pine forest. The Gladstones' idea is to mix tasteful and comfortable accommodation with private outdoor spaces for 'rewilding'. Their restored semi-detached six-sleeper North Lodge cottage, sitting pretty on the River Dye, has its own private path to the secluded woodland River Cabin, which is kitted out for a day spent mucking around outdoors. Go wild-river swimming, cook local sausages on a wood-burning stove, soak in a wood-fired Swedish

hot tub, or snuggle up on the couch in front of an open fire. The arrival hamper with bread, juice and shortbread, along with milk and eggs sourced from local farms, also includes, in true Scots style, whiskey.

....

-O- glendyecabinsandcottages.com

THE STARLIGHT ROOM 360°, ITALY

The cathedrals of rock and endless starry skies are your bedtime companions on a stay at the Starlight Room 360°. Sitting on the edge of a mountain ridge in Cortina d'Amprezzo, a ski resort in the Dolomites, Italy, this fir-timber hut makes good use of glass walls on three sides. It has a double bedroom with floor to ceiling views, a central bathroom and a cutesy dining room with red-cushioned built-in bench seats and a matching dining table. But the best bit? The 360 refers not just to the breathtaking unobstructed mountain views in every direction, but to the fact that the whole hut can swivel a complete 360 degrees. So you can dine while following the celestial movements of the night sky, then swivel the hut to continue the night show in bed. Stays are for one night only and include a warming alpine dinner beginning with hearty goulash and porcini soups, followed by typical mountain cold meats, cheeses and mustards washed down with Italian wine. Breakfast is at Rifugio Col Gallina, the main stone-and-wood alpine lodge that organises the stays.

....

-O- rifugiocolgallina.com/Eng/starlight-room-360.php

J.R.'S HUT, NEW SOUTH WALES, AUSTRALIA

There's an Australian folk song called 'The Road to Gundagai' and once it gets in your head it doesn't budge. But I digress. J.R.'s Hut is a splendiferous eco-hut plonked, rather daintily, on a hilltop at Kimo Estate near, you guessed it, Gundagai in New South Wales. Kimo (Ky-mo), an Indigenous word for 'mountains', is a working sheep and cattle farm. One of the oldest properties in this region, its history is filled with yarns about squatters, settlers and explorers. Adding to the story is a new generation putting weddings and accommodation on the agenda. The farm's accommodation includes two beautifully restored romantic old worker's cottages and the rusty, entirely loveable shearing shed, but J.R.'s Hut is where you'll feel the isolation. Architecturally designed, it seems inspired at once by both glamping (its triangular shape) and farm sheds (its timber frame and metal roof). Inside, it's like a boutique hotel — mid-century chairs, lovely linen, cable-knit throw rugs — but with a defiant off-grid remoteness thanks to its wood burner, tank water and 360-degree views shared between the bed and the front deck. Heaven.

....

-O- kimoestate.com/jrs-hut

BREWSTER HUT,
NEW ZEALAND

When it comes to huts, New Zealand walks the walk. The Department of Conservation manages a network of more than 950 huts catering to peripatetic adventurers across the country. Wherever you are in New Zealand, you can be certain there's a hut nearby. The huts vary from newly built, comfortable and sturdy (with functioning kitchens, heating, toilet facilities and 12 to 20 bunks with mattresses), to uninsulated wooden bivvies (providing basic shelter and zero facilities). All of the huts are bookable on a first-come, first-served basis, and they're happily cheap. Brewster Hut is located on the advanced Brewster Track in Mount Aspiring National Park in the Otago region. The tin shed, painted a bright post-box red, is a rare and beautiful sight standing alone on a flat ledge overlooking the valley and the endless snow-capped mountain peaks behind it. Inside, it's pine lined with 12 bunks, a large cooking area, a small bathroom, tank water (but no heating) and three tables of four so you can mingle with fellow hikers. Most visitors will set off early for the moon-lit two-hour climb to Mount Armstrong to see the sun kiss the mountain-tops pink, red and gold on rising.

-O- doc.gov.nz/parks-and-recreation/places-to-stay/ stay-in-a-hut

Wherever you are in New Zealand, you can be certain there's a hut nearby.

THE BEACH HUT, SOUTH DEVON, ENGLAND

Accessed via a steep cliff path and nestled in the kind of cove where a pirate might hide treasure, this hut in South Devon, England, is as romantic as it is secluded. It's built from local rocks and wood and has a shingled tile roof and heavy window shutters so that it fits snugly into the rugged rocky cliffs either side. Inside, it's a charmer with plenty of light, hammock seats for watching the seagulls, colourful cushions and, in the roof gable, a cosy double bed accessed via a ladder. There's no electricity, just solar-powered light, so on wintery weekends you can fire up the wood burner, which doubles as a hot-water boiler for enlivening outdoor showers. The small kitchen has all the basic amenities including a gas fridge, gas hob and sink with running water. There's also a barbecue and, in a separate shed, a composting toilet. The beach and sandy coastline are yours alone, as is the wood-fired outdoor hot tub from where you can watch for distant boats, listen to the waves roll in or keep an eye out for shooting stars. If the urge takes you, the local region is worth exploring. Head to Devon for eateries and shops or Newton Ferrers, a kilometre or so away, where you can hire a boat. You can also walk along the edge of Plymouth Sound to Cawsand and catch the passenger ferry back. If hiding away is your intention, your hosts can rustle up a food and wine hamper with goodies from nearby Devon. No need to leave. Ever.

....

-O- *hostunusual.com/categories/off-grid/the-beach-hut*

DIRECTION ISLAND BEACH SHACK, AUSTRALIA

Imagine this: it's just you, the vast ocean and this corrugated-iron beach shack, the sole structure on a tiny private island. This patch of wilderness, part of the Mackerel Islands, is 20 minutes by ferry from Onslow off the Western Australian coast. The shack, which looks like a typical Aussie shed, is simple but by no means rustic with a kitchen and dining area and two bedrooms with double beds and bunks. The bathroom is outdoors as is an upstairs dining area overlooking the sand dunes and the Indian Ocean. The kitchen has a stove, fridge, pots and pans and so on, but it is self-catered, so BYO (an Australian abbreviation for 'bring your own') groceries for kitchen cook-ups and outdoor barbecues. There's no aircon but there are ceiling fans and plenty of ocean breezes. Three-night minimum stays ensure you'll have time enough to explore the surrounding coral reef. Swim, snorkel, kayak, fish, birdwatch all the while keeping an eye out for marine visitors including passing whales, stingrays, fish, squid and tropical crays. Also recommended: 'catching up on that book you've been meaning to read' and recharging 'your batteries with some good music and chill time'.

-O- *mackerelislands.com.au*

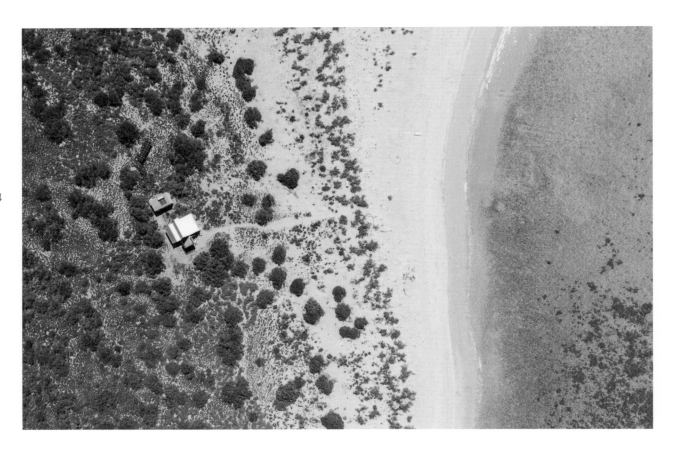

DUNTON HOT SPRINGS LOG CABINS, COLORADO, USA

Log cabin lovers will sink to their knees with one glimpse at Dunton Hot Springs, a resort resurrected from a romantic old mining town near Telluride, in the San Juan Mountains of the Colorado Rockies. Its 13 hand-hewn log cabins are handcrafted, in some cases by the original miners themselves. Carefully restored, with names such as Major Ross, Forge, Dunton Store and Echo, the cabins each have a distinct personality with unique decorations including rusted mining tools, animal pelt rugs, wooden lampshades, textured quilts, big baths and outdoor showers. All of them have the comforts and cosy essentials to see out the winter snow or summer alpine air. The cabins were built around the old dance hall and saloon, where guests now eat at a long antique table, a tradition from the big cattle outlaws. The 'ranch' is surrounded by pine-forested mountains and meadows along with a waterfall, an open-air chapel and, as the name suggests,

hot springs. You can relax in the mineral-rich waters inside the restored 19th-century bathhouse, in the pools, in the river and even in one of the cabins.

....

-O- *duntondestinations.com/hot-springs*

FOREST BATHING

'Thousands of tired, nerve-shaken, over-civilized people are beginning to find out that going to the mountains is going home; that wilderness is a necessity' – Scottish-born American naturalist John Muir stated this in his book *Our National Parks*, which was first published in 1901 to persuade readers that nature and national parks are essential not only for recreation but for health and wellbeing. More than a century later, it feels like the world might be finally catching up with Muir or, at least, certain trends point that way.

Japanese shinrin-yoku, or forest bathing, is one of them and, if you're not able to escape to a secluded bolthole, this could be an alternative refuge. According to Dr Qing Li in his book *Forest Bathing: How Trees Can Help You Find Health and Happiness*, the concept was developed in Japan in the 1980s to counter an over-worked population too commonly found asleep

at their desks. The research-based practice of creating physical and psychological wellness through immersion in forests and other natural environments actually became part of the country's public health program. Natural spaces around the country were designated as shinrin-yoku sites to enhance health, wellness and happiness.

There are countless studies to suggest that the slow act of mindfully walking along a forest path surrounded by birds and trees, clouds and butterflies, while intentionally engaging your five senses, leads to good things (such as improved memory, decreased anxiety, and high levels of positivity and sociability). But the science, as described by the Association of Nature and Forest Therapy, goes something like this: a 40-minute immersion in nature positively alters the biomarkers of stress and wellbeing. Heart rate and blood pressure decrease, levels of adrenaline and noradrenalin go down and parasympathetic nervous system activity increases. The upshot is improved mood and feelings of wellbeing, improved rest and energy levels, and decreased anxiety and depression. Together this helps immune function and mitigates the root cause of ailments such as heart problems, diabetes, skin conditions and weight gain to name a few.

We've known this for a while, apparently, but the real clincher is that recent evidence shows the natural phytoncides (oils secreted by evergreen trees) are for the most part responsible. So, a slow walk through a forest is in fact a chemical transaction between our bodies and the trees themselves. How poetic is that?

In his book *Your Guide to Forest Bathing*, M. Amos Clifford recommends you find a trained guide to help with the fundamentals and a familiar trail for consistent forest-bathing practice. But if, while travelling, you happen upon a walkable trail in a wooded environment (ideally with a mix of open areas, canopies and a natural water source), then you can try forest bathing. This is what Clifford recommends.

Arrive …
By noticing three things: the place you are in (look around and comment on what you notice), your body (become aware of how you are standing; pick up a stone and trace the movement as your turn it) and your senses (tune into them by standing in the one place for 15 minutes).

Walk slowly …
For 15 minutes while noticing what else is moving in the forest – bending grass, crawling insects.

Connect with the forest …
By noticing what draws your attention – a rock, tree or plant. Converse with it out loud, then thank it.

Find a sit spot …

And sit for 20 minutes to experience a 'slow reveal' when, perhaps, a shy animal pokes its nose out of a bush or inner stillness emerges.

Give back …

By noticing the natural world around you and acknowledging what you receive from it – shade, oxygen, peace. Offer something back, be it a thank-you gesture or even a song.

Dr Qing Li makes it even easier. He acknowledges that busy people might not have instant access to a wild nature spot. He suggests doing it in your own garden or local park as long as there is greenery around that you can connect to for inspiration. Take your shoes off and feel the grass under your feet, and, if you can walk, walk slowly. My tip? Leave your camera and your smart phone at home.

Discover more about forest bathing by visiting *natureandforesttherapy.org* and *forestbathing.info.*

Natural spaces around the country were designated as shinrin-yoku sites to enhance health, wellness and happiness.

Left and right: Forest walking in Japan's Yakushima National Park
Overleaf: Colorado's cosy log cabins (see p. 105)

ROADTRIPPING

Journeys by two wheels and four

A roadtrip is an archetypal adventure, a rite of passage, a bitumen right of way through uncharted terrain where it's possible to come out the other side having learned a little more about yourself. While roadtrips were traditionally the domain of four wheels, cyclists are increasingly taking up the mantle and venturing on backroads to rural and regional places where culture, history, people and landscape are accessible. While those in a vehicle share the camaraderie of a cabin, the flow of conversation, shared driving and somewhere to store the luggage, cyclists have the benefit of exercise, the sun on one's face and that free-wheeling feeling. Both slow travel modes enable authentic experiences in the landscape and its people.

Top: The epic Ruta 40 traverses stunning Argentinian scenery

Right top: Thai food on the Authentic South Thailand adventure

Right bottom: Cycle the road less travelled in Rwanda

When Swiss-born, Hong Kong–based Peter Schindler was getting his self-drive touring business On the Road Experiences up and running in China ten years ago, he invited me on a couple of his reconnaissance trips. The first had five of us squeezed into the back of a four-wheel drive on a two-week, 4000-kilometre (2485-mile) roadtrip through Sichuan and Yunnan. It was a wild old time – motorcycles, water buffalo, hand-pulled carts, rusty bicycles, scrawny chickens and pit stops in lands where few foreigners tread. The second trip was a shorter four days, beginning in Kunming and driving through Yunnan's green rice fields and past traditional Chinese architecture, snow-capped mountains, yaks, stupas and prayer flags to the Tibetan Plateau. Our final day took us to the remarkable muted-blue mountain chasm of the famed Tiger Leaping Gorge. It's a scene from an ancient Chinese painting that has stayed with me.

Schindler still offers guided self-driving tours into the heart of Tibet and Yunnan, and his business has grown to include itineraries in South-East Asia, Europe and Africa. The Myanmar trip in this chapter is another example of Schindler's forays into Asia's least explored backroads, and there are plenty of other operators who can help you get on the road.

Cyclists have the benefit of exercise, the sun on one's face and that free-wheeling feeling.

RUTA 40, ARGENTINA

Buckle up in the front for a bitumen adventure on one of the world's wildest, remotest and least travelled roads. RN40, Ruta 40 or La Cuarenta as it's known to Argentinians, is a 5000-kilometre (3100-mile) highway running alongside the Andes from Cabo Vírgenes, the southernmost point of the Argentine mainland, to northernmost Ciénaga, on the Bolivian border. It's as much a national icon as Route 66 in the USA, thanks largely to Ernesto Che Guevara whose famous *Motorcycle Diaries* narrative played out along much of the route. Swoop Patagonia's eight-day Infamous Route 40 itinerary begins in Bariloche, in Argentina's Lakes District, and crosses into Chile's remote southern region onto the Carretera Austral or 'Southern Road'. The detour – another awesome roadtrip – is where 'wild rivers flow through lush forests, rolling hills give way to snow-capped mountains, waterfalls tumble along steep cliff faces'. You'll stay in a coastal fishing village on the edge of the Chilean Fiords and hike to the Hanging Glacier in Queulat National Park. On day five you cross back into Argentina to hit the Ruta 40. Along it, you'll

stay in an estancia (ranch) and pit stop at Cueva de los Manos (Cave of the Hands), painted by the ancestors of the Tehuelche people (or Patagones) 3300 years ago. At the Los Glaciares National Park you'll see an ice field that lays claim to being the world's third largest reserve of fresh water.

....

-O- swoop-patagonia.com/tours/group/route-40-infamous

EXPERIENCE DEVON AND CORNWALL, ENGLAND

Leave your lycra at home; this resolutely relaxed bike ride through the charming English regions of Devon and Cornwall matches the laidback coastal ambience of the destinations themselves. Butterfield and Robinson's six-day itinerary is nicely padded with luxury heritage accommodation (including the terraced Hotel Tresanton, which sits seaside and overlooks Sir Anthony's Lighthouse) and the gamut of tempting eating venues, such as Rick Stein's restaurant in waterfront Padstow and a Brit pub in Chagford. Cultured encounters include a guided tour of the Tate St Ives (sister gallery to London's famous Tate Modern) and a visit to the Lost Gardens of Heligan, which were some of the finest gardens in the 1800s until they were left to grow wild after World War I. Adding to the relaxed vibe, you can punctuate the riding schedule with shorter distance options, 18 holes of golf, a stint of shopping or perhaps an afternoon tea. When not tempted off the bike, the cycling terrain is the rolling green-with-butterflies-and-blooms variety. You'll navigate quaint old former railway lines; pedal through the craggy landscape, moors and river valleys of Dartmoor (with its Bronze Age stone circles and Neolithic tombs); ride the magnificent Camel Trail along the Camel Estuary on Cornwall's north coast; and, after a ferry ride, cycle the coastal route to the 12th-century fishing town of Mevagissey. There's also a stint along Cornwall's coast-to-coast route to Portreath.

-O- butterfield.com/trip/devon-and-cornwall-biking

AUTHENTIC SOUTH THAILAND, THAILAND

Coconut trees, white sand, jungle greenery and tranquil lapping waters – riding through southern Thailand's dreamy beach-hopping scenery forms part of Spice Roads' 11-day cycle tour, but there's more. The itinerary also unlocks the authentic 'other' Thailand, a cultural mix of Thai Buddhist and Muslim seafarer traditions and history. The ride covers a total distance of 384 kilometres (176 miles) with eight days in the seat and an average distance of 48 kilometres (30 miles) per day. The route wends through quiet, shady rural roads, past beaches and rubber plantations, over river crossings and through fishing villages where leg stretches incorporate cave visits and roadside-stall snacking. You'll take a boat ride beneath towering karst cliffs to floating bamboo-bungalow accommodation on Cheow Laan Lake, and you'll ride on the edges of Khao Sok National Park – Thailand's last great rainforests alive with evergreens, limestone caves and wild animals. At Takua Pa you'll see traditional wooden buildings intermixed with Portuguese colonial buildings and, after a ferry ride to Koh Kho Khao Island, visit the Tsunami Victim Cemetery, which commemorates victims from 39 countries. The highlight is perhaps Koh Yao Noi Island, another boat ride away, where you'll explore the beach and bed down with a local fishing family in their traditional home.

-O- spiceroads.com/tours/souththailand/itinerary

A BURMESE JOURNEY, MYANMAR

Known as the Golden Lands, Myanmar's northern backroads are vivid and colourful and superb for eyeballing authentic Burmese day-to-day life. To get among it, On the Road Experiences' 12-day guided driving itinerary begins in Yangon with an hour-long flight north to Inle Lake, where floating gardens, stilt-top villages and crumbling stupas mark the start of the driving holiday. From here, memorable moments play out daily. At Inle Lake you'll take a longboat ride to see the famous leg-rowing technique of the lake's fishermen and in rural Pindaya you'll visit the Pindaya Cave, which is crammed with Buddha images and statues, stalagmites and stalactites. In Mandalay, Burma's last royal capital, you'll clock the 150-year-old Mahagandayon Monastery and famous U-Bein bridge, before continuing to the pilgrimage site atop extinct volcano Mount Popa and the magical

temples of Bagan. The journey ends at Ngapali, looking out at the Bay of Bengal. Driving days range from two to nine hours, the latter being a winding 235-kilometre (146-mile) drive across the Arakan Mountains. You'll be driving in a fully insured SUV, with the logistics (often complex in these parts) taken care of so all you have to do is keep your eye on the road (and the scenery).

....

-O- *ontheroadexperiences.com/en/destinations/burma*

VOLCANOS, LAKES AND GORILLAS, RWANDA

According to British humourist and slow cyclist Tim Moore, 'Slow and steady doesn't win the race. But it definitely has more fun along the way and comes home with better stories', and it's this mantra on which tour company The Slow Cyclist bases its tours. The group's seven-night cycling journey travels from the Rwandan capital, Kigali, in a north-west arc to the shores of one of Africa's Great Lakes, taking full advantage of the beguiling scenery in the 'Land of a Thousand Hills'. Pedallers ride between 32 kilometres (20 miles) and 80 kilometres (50 miles) on four of the eight days, with cultural and historical distractions along the way. In the capital you'll visit the Kigali Genocide Memorial (a harrowing but must-do Rwandan experience), the uplifting Kinamba Project and the Kimironko Market. Then you're in the saddle for some memorable riding: on day three you set off into the misty peaks from the top of Kigali's highest mountain, Mount Jali; on day four you descend through tea fields before the steady climb to the shores of the Twin Lakes, Ruhondo and Burera (where you'll stay in a convent with views towards the smoking, active Mount Nyiragongo volcano in the Congo); and on day seven you'll cycle along the base of the chain of volcanos, through bamboo forests, remote villages and banana plantations. One of the last rest stops is at the home of the late humanitarian and author Rosamond Carr. Electric bikes are a good option on some of the steeper terrain and, as they say, 'nobody has ever regretted taking one'.

....

-O- *theslowcyclist.co.uk/destinations/rwanda*

Slow cyclist

In late 2009 Oli Bloom was disillusioned with his nine-to-five job in London, so he quit, hopped on a bike and spent the next 14 months cycling to Australia to watch the Ashes cricket series. Along the way he played cricket in the shadow of Istanbul's Blue Mosque, slept in a goat pen in Sudan, battled sub-zero mountain temperatures in Bulgaria and successfully negotiated the treacherous highways of India. A book about his mad-cap adventures, *Cycling to the Ashes: A Cricketing Odyssey from London to Brisbane*, was published in 2014. By then Broom was enjoying a two-year stint in Rwanda where he was spending weekends exploring hidden corners of the country by bike. He returned home to the UK the following year intent on sharing his passion for cycling through some of the world's most beautiful places.

INTERVIEW:

OLI BROOM

His company, The Slow Cyclist, was born (*see* p. 115 for a Slow Cyclist trip). Whether guests like pottering along dusty backroads, inching up soaring mountains or winding through wildflower meadows, the Slow Cyclist mission is to offer incredible slow travel experiences. Guests can expect gourmet picnics in hilltop pastures; charming accommodation in homes, guest houses and farm stays; and total immersion in the country and its stories through expert encounters along the way, from botanists and ornithologists to historians and sommeliers.

You cottoned on to slow travel a while back, and now the rest of us are catching on. What's changing about the way travellers are approaching travel?

Travel is driven by the desire for authentic experiences these days. And they're difficult to find. People want to get under the skin of a place – they don't want to eat in restaurants; they want to eat home-cooked food in a local home. They don't want to watch a local dance troupe; they want to drink and dance with them.

Inspiration behind Slow Cyclist's journey formats?

We wanted to offer a holiday that was long enough for our guests to feel like they were escaping reality, but short enough that it wasn't a huge decision to travel … Five nights is the perfect length. Guests feel like they've been away for much longer. It's a function of being on the move and seeing new things all day, every day.

About your incredible roadtrip to Australia: best slow travel moment?

This is a tricky one, as the whole trip was slow travel. Watching the landscape change slowly – almost surreptitiously – under my wheels was a great pleasure. Wild swimming was always a treat – I spent hours swimming alone in outback billabongs, being careful to avoid the saltwater crocodiles!

The ride made me conscious of how good humans are at adapting to their surroundings. It also acted as a good reminder that whoever you are – whether you live on an outback cattle station, in a Kolkatan palace or a Sudanese mud hut – when it comes down to it, we all want little more than happiness and health for our families.

The experiences made me a lot more trusting of people. All across the globe, I had so many uplifting experiences with complete strangers that reaffirmed my faith in humans.

Where's your slow place now?

My wife and I got married in a village outside Cahors in south-west France. We return for at least a week every year. The roads are practically empty, so bike rides are glorious, there are very few tourists, and the pace of life is perfect.

I also love Mesendorf, a village in Transylvania that many of our Slow Cyclist guests visit. I have spent around a year of the past four years there. It's the most magical village I've ever been to and the hill above the village, behind the house I rented for six months, is most definitely my happy place.

Advice for travellers wanting slow?

It can be hard for busy minds to settle into slow ways, but we find those travellers get the most out of the journey. I don't have a mantra, but I do like to say that our journeys are perfect for curious travellers with a bit of juice in their legs. They are people who want to see new places, but don't want to be stuck behind a car windscreen. This is the essence of the Slow Cyclist.

Overleaf: The slow-going coastal route on the cycle journey through Devon and Cornwall (see p. 113)

CULTURAL IMMERSION

Getting deep on people and place

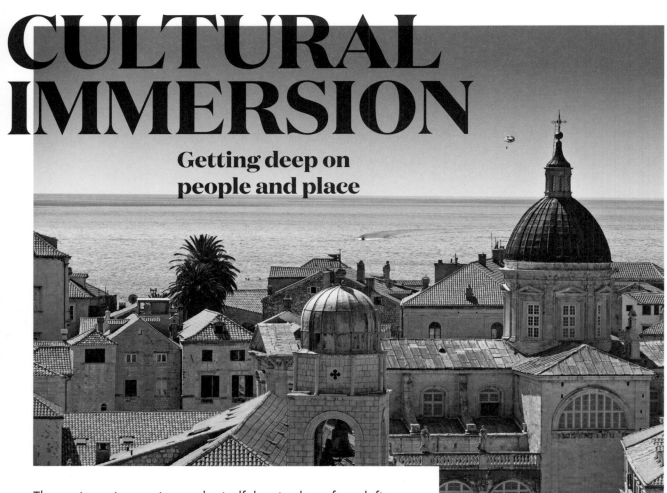

The curious, immersive and mindful traits that often define slow travel are felt most intensely when you're tapping into a combination of authentic places and the real-life local people who inhabit them. Whether it's in the warmth of a rural kitchen cooking with a nonna, on a national park field trip with a university professor, or on a visit to a refugee camp with a top journalist, immersion brings engagement and connection with it.

One of my favourite slow experiences as a backpacker was a week spent in the languid heat on the Dalmatian coast in Croatia. Our group of five 20-somethings had chanced upon guesthouse accommodation in the simple beachfront home of a woman called Magda. I'd been instantly drawn to her because she reminded me of my mum. Blonde hair swept up on the top of her head in a messy bun and apron permanently around her waist. She also gave us the mum-like hearty welcome of a people-person who is happy when there's food to be cooked and plenty of people around the table.

Top: Explore historic Dubrovnik on the Local Living Croatia experience

Right top: Ad Deir (the Monastery) in the ancient metropolis of Petra, Jordan

Right bottom: A welcome from the women's cooperative on the Medinas To Mountains tour in Morocco

We planned to be at Magda's for one night but ended up staying for a week. We ventured on little side trips into Dubrovnik to explore the old town, but the real travel experiences happened sitting at Magda's al fresco wooden dining table, which was shaded by a fig tree that would punctuate conversations by landing its big, fat, milky fruit on one of our dinner plates. Magda's husband, whose name I have forgotten, would push his dinghy out each morning, and Magda would slap his catch – a fish or a squid – in a fry pan with a squeeze of lemon picked from her orchard and serve it with a salad of vegetables delivered from a neighbour's garden.

With food as communion and Magda's rather tart homemade wine as the lubricant, we travellers would share stories about each other's countries and cultures, politics and private lives, loves and losses. When we weren't having deep-and-meaningfuls around the table or helping Magda in the kitchen, we'd be rocking in hammocks, reading tattered books that had done the rounds of the hostel community and taking walks as the sunlight faded over the Adriatic.

You can rely on the serendipitous nature of travel for these kinds of experiences, but I love that the slow travel trend sees these kinds of holidays consciously factored into itineraries. The Local Living Croatia experience in this chapter reminded me of my trip. The others touch a chord too.

LOCAL LIVING, CROATIA

Your base on this week-long stint just near Dubrovnik on Croatia's southern Dalmatian coast is a lovely rural Mediterranean homestead, or agroturizam, with rustic terracotta charm and views over the Konavle Valley and the Adriatic Sea. G Adventures' new Local Living itineraries aim to settle guests in a down-to-earth environment among, in this case, real Croatians, so you can get a feel for their way of life. For this southern Dalmatian itinerary you'll be based in the beautiful green-swept and coastal town of Lovorno, which is handy for exploring the region south of Dubrovnik. You'll hit up Dubrovnik itself with a local guide giving you the low-down on the historic walled city, and spend a day swimming and boating between Molunat and Prevlaka with an afternoon at a secluded beach. Other trip highlights include biking on a scenic cycle route through Lovorno's rolling vineyards and stopping by a local artist's residence, a 15th-century monastery and a quaint flour mill along the way. You'll also take a tour through nearby Konavle's wineries, which are well known for their prosecco, olive oil and wine production (and a taste-test or two). Chill time is villa time. Hang on the outdoor terrace to take in the views or swim in the pool. Your hosts, the Mujo family who reside next door, will be on-hand with local expertise, and the doyenne, Grandma Mujo, hosts a cooking class using fresh ingredients from the neighbours and the farm. Naturally, you get to eat it afterwards around the dinner table with the whole family. A beautiful immersive experience.

-O- gadventures.com.au/trips/local-living-croatia-southern-dalmatia/ECDL

STUDY GEOLOGY AT UNIVERSITY OF MONTANA WESTERN, USA

Rock-hopping natural-world boffins, pack your bags for a campus-based three-week educational experience taught by an adjunct instructor of geology at University of Montana Western. Roads Scholar's new and engrossing 21-day itinerary explores the rich railroading and mining history, geology and ecology of the Northern Rocky Mountains region and Yellowstone National Park. The course combines scientific and creative pursuits with a combination of lab time, studio time and fieldwork. After the initial university orientation, where a group leader and naturalist will discuss roles, responsibilities and practicalities for your stay, it will be time to hit the books. You'll be guided through a discovery of the Rocky Mountain ecosystem and learn about environmental science and the local geology. Then you're in the studio for sessions with an artist and educator who will introduce geo-scientist techniques for observational journalling and sketching, a tool that will go hand-in-hand with your scientific notes. Armed with the basics you'll take the classroom outdoors and into the field. You'll explore many facets of America's first national park, the 8991-square-kilometre (3471-square-mile) Yellowstone National Park, an exquisite land of valleys, canyons, rivers, lakes and mountain ranges. Highlights include visits to Mammoth Hot Springs and the Heritage and Research Centre, which houses the 5.3-million-item Yellowstone Archive. You'll also explore the park's Grand Canyon and experience the roar of the mighty Upper Falls.

-O- roadscholar.org/find-an-adventure

TRAVEL FOR THE MIND WITH GEORGE NEGUS, JORDAN, ISRAEL AND THE OCCUPIED TERRITORIES

Veteran journalist, author, TV presenter and Australian household name George Negus is the VIP escort for World Expeditions' 14-day delve into Jordan, Israel and the Occupied Territories. His 30-something years covering the Middle East and its complex global politics have provided him with encyclopaedic knowledge of the region and a wealth of contacts and friendships. You'll be tapping into all three on an immersive itinerary that begins in Amman, the capital of Jordan, then heads north to Jerash, west to Jerusalem and Tel Aviv, then loops down to the south of Jordan and back north to Amman. The itinerary ticks off some seriously beautiful places including two of my favourites: Petra, the ancient metropolis carved into red desert sandstone rocks, and Wadi Rum, Jordan's magical star-strewn, big-skied desert where you'll sleep in a Bedouin tent. You'll also take a dip in the Dead Sea, which lies 400 metres (1312 feet) below sea level (floating is easy, just don't open your eyes under water

like I did), and explore the old biblical city of Jerusalem. Then there's the intellectually stimulating angle – the chance to get below the surface on some regional issues. You'll spend time (unobserved) at Jordan's Zaatari Refugee Camp, where an estimated 80,000 people live in tents or shipping containers. In Israel and the Occupied Territories you'll meet a United Nations expert whose subject is the notorious Separation Wall, which Negus describes as 'an impossible-to-ignore wall-cum-cage 8 metres (26 feet) high and currently 650 kilometres (404 miles) long'. You'll stay in local hotels and get your fill of the Middle East's distinctive spicy cuisine. The trip often times with the closing days of Ramadan, the Middle East's month of fasting.

....

-O- worldexpeditions.com/Israel/Adventure-Touring/ Travel-for-the-Mind-Jordan-Israel-and-the-Occupied- Territories-with-George-Negus

Cultural immersion

123

MEDINAS TO MOUNTAINS, MOROCCO

Solo travel is another recent trend whereby travellers going it alone can sign up to tours and experiences with other fancy-free people. An off-shoot of this trend is solo female travel, and Wild Women Expeditions is on to it. Its Medinas to Mountains of Northern Morocco 10-day women-only itinerary delves into the Berber culture of the women of Morocco, which is known in the region for its support for women's rights. On the other hand, over 80 per cent of women are illiterate. To help gain an insight into the lives of local women, the itinerary works with female Berber entrepreneurs who own their transport and drive their own vehicles. You'll also have Berber women tour guides. The tour begins in Casablanca where you spend three days exploring Hassan II Mosque, one of the largest mosques in the world admired for its intricately carved marble and mosaics and extensive glass floor that can hold over 24,000 worshippers. You'll visit the magnificent old medina of Fez, a World Heritage site, and labyrinthine streets with mosques, mausoleums, madrasas and hammams. In the mountains and countryside, you'll go horseriding in Meknes, stop by Moulay Idriss, the oldest town in Morocco, and stay in a riad in Chefchaouen, known as 'the blue city' for its blue-washed buildings (with red-tiled roofs). You'll feast with a rural family, prepare a Moroccan tagine, and hike to Akchour Waterfalls to swim in the freshwater pools below. In Marrakech guests can gawp at Jemaa el Fna, the city's chaotic market square, which is UNESCO-listed for Intangible Cultural Heritage. You'll also visit women's cooperatives and stay in another riad, this time one that employs those trained by the Amal Centre for disadvantaged women.

....

-O- wildwomenexpeditions.com/trips/medinas-to-mountains-northern-morocco

CREATIVE WRITING IN THE COTSWOLDS, ENGLAND

C.S. Lewis and J.R.R. Tolkien first talked about their enchanted worlds – Narnia and Middle-earth respectively – over a warm ale at a pub in Oxford. Or at least that's how the story goes. Happily, stories are what this cultural immersion is about. Better Read Literary Tours' Creative Writing in the Cotswolds itinerary is a seven-day retreat in one of England's most charming and historic regions replete with glorious old gardens, romantic castles, yew mazes and mysterious circles of standing stones. It's home to both Oxford, of the eponymous prestigious university and nicknamed the 'city of dreaming spires' for its historic cathedrals and colleges, and Stratford-upon-Avon, the gorgeous riverside town whose former residents include one William Shakespeare (the Bard). The Cotswolds landscape has inspired many famous authors, including Kate Forsyth who wrote her first novel at the age of seven and now, with 40 books to her name, has sold more than a million copies globally. Writers at any stage of their career will spend the mornings with Forsyth learning the key conventions of popular literary genres including historical fiction, crime and mystery, romance, horror, fantasy and magic realism, while picking up tips on rules, research, structure, patterns, voice, suspense and surprise. In the afternoons, you'll further inspire your creative reflexes by exploring the locale with activities such as a private tour of the 15th-century house where Shakespeare was born and a tour of Oxford University. The esteemed university is the alma mater of 13 British prime ministers and its Great Hall is the model for Harry Potter's Hogwarts school. You'll stay at the Tudor Shakespeare Hotel in Stratford-upon-Avon. For further literary immersion combine the experience with the UK's Historical Novel Society conference and Edinburgh International Book Festival (in 2020) or Shakespeare's birthday activities (in 2021).

....

-O- *betterreadtours.com/creativewriting*

Cultural immersion

125

SKILL SET

Honing your skills, crafts or interests is another means of getting under the skin of a destination – its people, history, culture and traditions – more deeply and thoughtfully. This could be on a three-hour architecture tour in Buenos Aires or an eight-day field and photography adventure in Bhutan. Find your talent, zone in on your destination and seek out the expert. Or the other way around.

BUENOS AIRES ARCHITECTURE TOUR, ARGENTINA

Buenos Aires, the Argentinian capital, draws much of its complex present-day identity from its golden age – or Belle Époque – at the beginning of the 20th century. Context Travel's three-hour tour, led by a local architect or urban historian, explores the history and politics of this era through the city's civil and private architecture. You'll walk the Avenida de Mayo, past the National Congress, and visit the famous Teatro Colón and stunning Palacio Barolo – possibly the best example of the era's wealth. Then you'll stroll through the Recoleta and Retiro neighbourhoods: past the private palaces of Argentine high society along Avenida Alvear and through Plaza Pellegrini and Plaza San Martín.

....

-O- contexttravel.com

126

COWBELL CASTING, SWITZERLAND

Bell casting, in the town of Berger in the Emmental region of Bärau, is as much a part of Swiss identity as gruyere cheese. Centuries ago bells were used to keep tabs on roaming cattle and today they ring out at local festivities. The Berger Swissbell Foundry has been casting bells since 1730 and the tradition and quality have been maintained. Try your hand at casting a bell in the foundry's half-day workshops. You'll learn about the foundry's history, then you can choose a cow bell, sheep bell, goat bell, house bell or ship's bell (the list goes on) before filling the moulds with metal heated to 1100 degrees Celsius (2012 degrees Fahrenheit). When molten, the bells are then cast and finished with a matching strap. The perfect souvenir.

....

-O- swissbells.com/the-seminars

HIMALAYAN FILM AND PHOTOGRAPHY EXPEDITION, BHUTAN

Shooting on old-fashioned film requires photographers to 'capture their surroundings with deliberation and intention … for more intimate visual illustrations'. So says award-wining photographer Michael Turek who leads this eight-day Como Hotels itinerary through three photogenic regions of Bhutan, the intriguing landlocked Buddhist country with a monarchy. Through the lens of your camera you'll see the capital of Thimphu with its gold-topped Buddhist dzongs; Punakha Valley known for its religious festivals; and the rice paddy valley of Paro, home to cliff-clinging Tiger's Nest Monastery, one of the highlights of the trip.

....

-O- comohotels.com/en/umaparo/offers/eight-day-himalayan-photography-expedition-michael-turek

Left: The National Congress in Buenos Aires
Right: An artisan at work in Florence

HILL AND MOUNTAIN SKILLS, ALBANIA, KOSOVO AND MACEDONIA

The Šar Mountains wilderness extends through the Balkans from Kosovo through the north-west of North Macedonia to north-eastern Albania. In this hardy terrain, adventurers on Secret Compass' nine-day comprehensive hill and mountain skills training course will, with the help of professional mountaineers, master navigation, campcraft, route planning, wilderness first-aid, river crossing techniques, mountain weather systems and environmental impact mitigation. The aim is to be capable of self-supported treks and hill adventures. You'll be active for up to nine hours per day for seven consecutive days, carrying up to 20 kilograms (45 pounds) per person. The highlight will be trekking a section of the 495-kilometre (308-mile) High Scardus Trail, which includes a summit assault of Mount Korab (2764 metres; 9068 feet).

-O- *secretcompass.com/expedition/balkans-expedition-skills-beyond-borders*

FLORENCE ARTISAN WORKSHOP TOUR, ITALY

Home to artisans for the past 500 years, Florence's Oltrano neighbourhood is a maze of intricate side streets lined with small workshops where leatherworkers, silversmiths, shoemakers and milliners still ply their historic trades. On Context Travel's three-hour tour you visit some of these workshops to observe the craftspeople in action. A local scholar and docent will describe the traditional processes practised by each artist and discuss the traditions, value and role of manufacturing in Italian culture. The emphasis here is on the importance of preserving and promoting these dying arts – slow traditions in a world that often feels inundated with mechanical and digital technology.

-O- *contexttravel.com/cities/florence/tours/made-in-florence-oltrarno-artisans*

RIDE LIKE A COWBOY, USA

The 1990s comedy movie *City Slickers* has a similar premise to this half- or full-day Abercrombie and Kent itinerary – ditching the office and your devices for a wrangling adventure in the Arizona desert. Whatever your ability, you'll don a Stetson and leather chaps and, with the guidance of real wild west cowboys and expert wranglers, jump in the saddle for cowboy college 101. You'll get tips on riding western style, learn rope skills (like how to swing a lasso), and get the low-down on horse-shoeing and animal body language. Seasoned riders can brush up their jumping skills before riding through the cactus-strewn desert known for its iconic sights: Monument Valley, the Grand Canyon and Cathedral Rock.

-O- *abercrombiekent.co.uk/destinations/north-america/usa/utah-and-arizona/ride-like-a-cowboy*

Traveller and social entrepreneur

Entrepreneur, leader, philanthropist and author Bruce Poon Tip is the Canadian founder of G Adventures, a small group adventure travel company and social enterprise. After returning from a backpacking tour of Asia in 1990, Poon Tip was driven to share his passion for experiencing adventures in an authentic and sustainable way. With nothing more than Poon Tip's own personal credit cards, G Adventures was born. It has since grown from a one-man show into a company with more than 2200 employees in 28 offices worldwide, and from a handful of trips in Latin America to more than 700 adventures across all seven continents. Poon Tip's first book, *Looptail: How One Company Changed the World by Reinventing Business*, was released in 2013 and became a *New York Times* bestseller.

INTERVIEW:

Bruce Poon Tip

Overleaf: The landscape of the Northern Rocky Mountains region, Montana (see p. 122)

In 2018 he was named Canada's Most Admired CEO in the category of social entrepreneurship. His Planeterra Foundation, which connects local communities with tourism by developing and supporting community-owned enterprises, has projects in 42 countries. It is this vision for preserving cultural heritage and conserving and replenishing the natural environment – while also improving the lives of local people – that deeply resonates with today's travellers.

What's changing about the way travellers are approaching their next destination?

I think that people are living differently at home. People are eating organic food, considering their food miles (for example, the 100-mile diet) and recycling as much as possible – as a result of this increased awareness, people are matching their travel more with their values. I think when people book a cruise or a compound kind of resort holiday, the destination is irrelevant – they're shopping on price or dates that match and they suspend their usual beliefs that they live by at home. Now, however, we see people trying to connect their values with how they travel. And I believe there will be a tipping point where more and more people will think it's weird that they're within the walls of a resort with thousands of others consuming massive amounts of natural resources when, just outside those walls, people don't have clean drinking water or access to medical care. There will come a point where people find that odd.

What was the inspiration behind G Adventures' new wellness trips?

Whether it impacts us directly or remotely, someone we know or ourselves, we are all affected somehow by mental illness. So wellness has become something that's critical for people within their work, within their life; it's a challenge for us as an employer to create an environment where people can achieve wellness at work and combine that into their lives. By extension we're hoping they'll want to incorporate it into their holidays because people are making it a priority for their own wellbeing. People are more focused on taking care of themselves and wanting to do it in a way that benefits others. Our model has always been about having a positive impact when you travel, so it's kind of a full loop for us: it's about taking care of yourself, but knowing if you do it in our style you can also positively affect local communities.

And the Local Living trips you now offer?

Community tourism is really new for us and we want to own that space. It's taking people to areas that aren't tourist attractions, places where it's more of a cultural immersion experience where local people who wouldn't normally have tourists visit actually benefit. And it's about getting the ultimate in an authentic experience because that is the epitome of slow travel. Staying with local families, staying on a ranch, staying with a nomadic tribe in inner Mongolia or with a tribe in the Amazon – that's the experience we want Local Living travellers to have.

Memorable slow travel moments?

I think these moments tend to be in very remote areas. The two that come to mind in particular are Tibet and Mongolia where the beauty is more of a stark beauty – you're not chasing any of kind of big tourist attraction. It's a spiritual experience and it's also very rough terrain. You're travelling where there's no infrastructure, so quite often you're delayed or you're held up in a place because of weather conditions (especially in Tibet) like snow storms or not being able to cross a pass. Those kind of experiences have become much more critical for me as I get older – that is, there's more of a spiritual connection within yourself and with the region. Also, you have a better understanding of yourself as a result of travelling to nourish the soul as opposed to simply chasing a bucket list.

Advice for travellers wanting to slow down?

I think there are many ways in which we should slow down but the first one is about getting disconnected. I mean, I'm amazed at the number of people still wanting wifi on trips, still wanting to be connected. We have to offer this, because the way people are holidaying these days is that they can't relax unless they're socially connected. But for people to have a deeply immersive experience, I believe they must be able to disconnect. Because we live in such a wired world there's this premium on being available all the time. I think we have to find ways in which we can truly get away. And that doesn't necessarily mean not having a phone or taking pictures along the way, but rather making sure we take digital breaks and don't just see or experience culture through a camera or social media.

TIME IT RIGHT

Natural phenomena and seasonal journeys

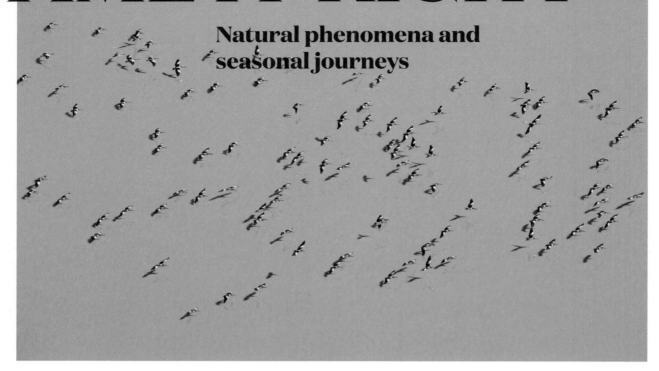

Budget airlines and cheap flights have revolutionised travel by putting the world at our fingertips at prices most people can afford. At the cost of service, and often a smile, we can be a long way away from the everyday in the blink of an eye. There is a pay-off of course. Destinations at the end of cheap flights are often over-crowded, mostly with people from the place you were trying to get away from. Public transport from minor airports can be unreliable, if it exists at all, and taxis are often expensive; taking off and landing times are usually off-peak and flight cancellations are common. I once bought a £36 return flight from London's Stansted Airport to Granada in Spain. The flight arrived back in London long after the last train had departed and the black cab home cost me £98, more than double the price of the air fare. It was a lesson well learnt. Buying cheap flights can be a reactive decision too. The cheap flight is flashed up on our feed, and we buy before we miss out on an impossibly good deal.

Top: Bird life at South Australia's Kati Thanda–Lake Eyre

Right top: On the way to the summit of Japan's iconic Mount Fuji

Right bottom: Sanctuary Kusini Camp, Tanzania

132

Some of the world's richest experiences can occur in unexpected locations at inconvenient times ...

What we actually miss out on is the mindfulness of careful planning, the excitement of looking forward to an adventure, the satisfaction of preparing for a trip and the sense of achievement when we finally arrive. This type of journey planning can make slow travel even more gratifying and fulfilling, particularly if you want to time your travel with a special event. It might be a naturally occurring phenomenon that requires research ahead of time, or a seasonal adventure that requires thinking ahead and booking long before you set off. Some of the world's richest experiences can occur in unexpected locations at inconvenient times so planning is essential, and the rewards speak for themselves.

A total solar eclipse is a rare and special experience – and so is a trip to Antarctica. The combination of the two makes Aurora Expeditions' special 22-night solar eclipse itinerary a once-in-a-lifetime voyage. A total solar eclipse occurs only every one to two years and, according to NASA, the solar eclipse on 4 December 2021 will be visible from Antarctica, South Africa and the South Atlantic. But the full solar eclipse – when the new moon passes between the sun and the Earth, totally blocking out the sun – will only be visible from Antarctica. You'll be in the most favourable position to see it on the *Greg Mortimer* ship, which will be berthed in the Weddell Sea south-east of the Antarctica peninsula. All you will need are clear skies and favourable weather conditions. The eclipse is on day 11 of the voyage. Either side of the big event you'll explore the incredible white continent, spotting icebergs, photographing nest-building Adélie penguins and peering at orca whales through binoculars. Other highlights include kayaking and snowshoeing. On the return journey you'll explore South Georgia, the end-of-the-Earth home to elephant seals, fur seals, wandering albatross and some of the largest king penguin colonies on the planet. Need more time to plan? The next total solar eclipse in this part of the world happens in April 2023.

SOLAR ECLIPSE, ANTARCTICA

....

 auroraexpeditions.com.au/expedition/solar-eclipse
 timeanddate.com/eclipse/list.html

HANG SON DOONG CAVES, VIETNAM

You could fly a Boeing 747 through the largest passageway in Vietnam's Son Doong Cave, a visual that gives you some idea of how big the world's largest cave really is. Located in the heart of the Phong Nha Ke Bang National Park in central Vietnam's Quang Binh province, this natural wonder only opened to the public in 2013. And with only one operator conducting tours, and a cap on the number of tourists each year (500), it has become something of a rite of passage for caving adventurers. Oxalis Adventure Tours' four-day itinerary (in partnership with the British Cave Research Association and the Vietnam Government) takes you into the depths of this strange alien world populated by enormous stalactites and stalagmites, an underground river, bizarre creepy-crawlies, sun-less gardens and tennis-ball–sized calcium deposits known as 'cave pearls'. The trip is difficult and you'll need to be fit to cope with 25 kilometres (16 miles) of jungle trekking and 9 kilometres (6 miles) of caving including rope climbs, rocky terrain, bouldering and scrambling ascents. But you'll be fully immersed, camping for two nights in Son Doong Cave and one night at Hang En Cave. Other memorable moments include visiting Ban Doong ethnic minority village, ascending the 90-metre (295-foot) Great Wall of Vietnam, and setting eyes on Green Gours, a cave opening with a paradisiacal garden lit by celestial shards of sunlight.

-O- oxalis.com.vn/tour/son-doong-cave-expedition-4d3n

THE GREAT MIGRATION, TANZANIA

The southern Serengeti National Park is parched and desolate at the start of November, a vast savannah seemingly devoid of wildlife and water. But sometime within the month following (the precise time varies each year), the treeless grasslands come alive with the buds and blooms that accompany falling rains. Then the wildlife follows. This is the home of the Great Migration when more than 1.5 million wildebeest and a quarter of a million zebra head towards their calving grounds in the south of the Serengeti. With them come the big five: lions, leopards, elephants, buffalo and rhino and their entourage – gazelles, giraffes, waterbucks, hippo, warthogs, impalas and dik diks. One day might look like a veritable Noah's ark of animals, the next you might only see zebras far on the horizon. On a rocky outcrop overlooking the southern plains, Sanctuary Kusini Camp is the only permanent camp in this remote part of Tanzania. Twelve safari tents, each with private wooden verandah, are nestled amid the acacias, creating perfect viewing platforms to sit back and watch as the animals, from December through March, congregate right at the camp's doorstep. As the Kusini team describe it: 'Lions survey the plains from their strategic vantage point … ghostly leopards lie in wait, cheetahs steer clear of the chaos and take refuge in the rolling vast savannah. And, of course, large clans of ever-present hyena roam in search of the weak, the wounded, and the ill.' Wildlife at its evolutionary best.

-O- sanctuaryretreats.com/tanzania-camps-kusini

MOUNT FUJI'S SUMMIT, JAPAN

There's a Japanese proverb that says, 'A wise man climbs Fuji once. A fool climbs it twice', which is to say this is a rather difficult undertaking and once in a lifetime is enough. The glorious snow-capped Fuji-san – a currently dormant volcano – is a near-symmetrical triangle, an extraordinary cloud-kissing solo peak so jaw-droppingly lovely it graces many a guidebook as Japan's most recognisable icon. It is located about 100 kilometres (62 miles) south-west of Tokyo. The summit is 3776 metres (12,388 feet) above sea level and marks the highest point of Japan, so getting to the top requires some planning. The official climbing season is restricted to just two months of the year, from 1 July to 31 August (although many of the mountain huts stay open a few weeks either side of these dates). This timeframe rules out visiting during the country's popular cherry-blossom season in spring, but it doesn't stop the devoted. Every year about 200,000 people (30 per cent are foreigners) set out to conquer the summit on one of four routes: Kawaguchiko, Subashiri, Gotemba and Fujinomiya. From the fifth station (which you can climb or bus to) it will take about six hours to clamber to the summit, but if, like most people, you want to see the sunrise, you'll be climbing in the dark in below-freezing temperatures with the threat of storms. Amateur climbers can book a room in a mountain hut for a nap and meal mid-hike, or you can forgo the sunrise and enjoy a daylight hike with fewer people. Whether you're a wise man or a fool, you'll never forget that view from the rooftop of Japan.

....

-O- *fujisan-climb.jp/en*

KATI THANDA–LAKE EYRE, AUSTRALIA

Colonially known as Lake Eyre (with the Indigenous name of the Arabana language added only recently), Kati Thanda is a South Australian outback phenomenon, a lake that only sees water every three to ten years and only completely floods around three times every 160 years. When the lake's water level is low, its glittering crystallised surface stretches beyond the arid desert dunes and salty claypans as far as the eye can see. When the desert downpours do come, it's almost biblical: the land transforms into a spectacular colourful oasis, a festival of wildlife and flora. Waterbirds descend in their thousands, fish converge in rivulets and channels and wildflowers bloom across the floodplains. The flat saltpan can fill to 9500 square kilometres (3668 square miles), making it, on these very rare occasions, the biggest lake in Australia. And at approximately 15 metres (49 feet) below sea level – the lowest natural point on the continent – it's as salty as the sea. When the water begins to evaporate, the lake takes on a spectacular pink hue caused by a pigment found within a salt-loving algae. This is when it's at its most memorable. Air Adventure's three-day Lake Eyre, Dig

Tree and the Prairie air safaris feature scenic flights over Cooper Creek, Warburton Groove, Coongie Lakes, Lake Eyre North and South, Belt Bay and Jackboot Bay. The most recent flooding was in 2019, with water from floods in Queensland slowly flowing over 1000 kilometres (621 miles) into Lake Eyre North.

....

-O- airadventure.com.au/lake-eyre-tours
-O- southaustralia.com/travel-blog/kati-thanda-lake-eyre

Overleaf: Kati Thanda–Lake Eyre, South Australia

SLOW FOOD

Culinary travels
and adventures

Italy's slow food movement is like the nonna of slow travel.
It started in 1986 when a group of like-minded individuals
countered the arrival of a certain fast food chain with a slow
food movement. Somewhat ironically, the concept spread
around the globe quickly. Since the slow food movement, the
West in particular has seen a sourcing, eating and dining
revolution amplified by 'craft', 'boutique', 'artisan' and
'hipster' trends. Barista coffee is the norm, food trucks are a
thing and farmers' markets have sprouted like mung beans.
Health and nutrition are on the menu, vegetarianism has
gone mainstream and vegans actually have menu options.
We've learned to activate our almonds and whizz up kale
smoothies and we expect our char-grilled brussels sprouts
to be garnished – at very least – with roasted pepitas and
foraged micro herbs.

Top: Fresh Tuscan olives, Italy

*Right top and bottom: Foraging on the Lapland
adventure, Sweden*

This foodie obsession has filtered into the travel sector. A decade ago, cooking classes in Thailand and Vietnam were a hit. You'd spend the morning in the local market looking for exotic ingredients, then learn to prep and roll your own rice paper rolls and make noodle salad before tucking in. Today this kind of interaction has, happily, been expanded with celebrity chefs as tour guides and multi-day itineraries styled specifically to connect travellers with local chefs and cooks. You can embrace regional recipes and cooking techniques and plunge the fork deeper to taste-test the role of cuisine through the history and culture of a region.

On a food trip in India many moons ago, I bemoaned the fact that our guide would sit at a nearby table and eat his own version of the local cuisine while we ate the spiced-down foreigner version. Now, it's more likely we'd be eating the guide's version, and we'd probably be eating it around the dining table with his family. That's connection through food.

LOCAL LIVING, ITALY

There's no escaping the food culture in Italy – or perhaps the food culture is the escape. G Adventures' Local Living itineraries include two culinary destinations that make choosing where to go that little bit harder. The seven-day Coastal Tuscany itinerary begins and ends in Rome. In between, you'll head north up the coast to unpack your bags at a quaint Tuscan hillside villa. Here you'll sample homemade olive oil pressed in local groves (with a side of Tuscan bread) and visit a neighbouring winery before sitting down to your first home-cooked dinner. With the villa as your base, you can explore the streets of Capalbio, a remarkably well-preserved medieval town, and head further afield under your own steam on a trip to the Etruscan town of Pitigliano. Or opt for a bike ride to Feniglia beach or a visit to the archaeological site of Cosa to soak in the local hot springs. There's a day set aside for exploring the nearby island of Monte Argentario, where you can wander around the port villages, take a hike in the Tuscan hillside, or spend the day snorkelling in the Tyrrhenian Sea. The seven-day Sorrento itinerary starts and ends in Naples, but you'll spend the time in between unwinding on an organic lemon farm, or agriturismo, with a local family as your hosts. You'll take a tour of the property and get the intel on lemon cultivation before being shown how the famous limoncello liquor is made. You'll also learn to make that famous Naples staple – pizza. Side trips include the Path of the Gods trail along the Amalfi Coast past lemon groves, woodland and abandoned farmhouses. Also included are a ferry ride to the island of Capri, home of the Caprese salad, and a guided tour of Pompeii.

-O- gadventures.com.au/trips/local-living-italy-sorrento/5543
-O- gadventures.com.au/trips/local-living-italy-coastal-tuscany/5952

NORTHERN FOOD TRAILS WITH PETER KURUVITA, SRI LANKA

Australian chef, television personality and author Peter Kuruvita credits his childhood spent cooking with his grandmother in the traditional kitchen of his ancestral home in Colombo, Sri Lanka, as inspiration not only for his first cookbook, but also for his long-standing career. The latest incarnation of which is as host on World Expeditions' 16-day foodie itinerary that includes the little-visited north-east of Sri Lanka. The trip starts in Colombo where you'll explore the night food stalls and Lellama fish market. You'll then head north on a loop that takes in the palm-fringed west coast through Wilpatthu National Park to Jaffna with its fort and ramparts and Tamil culture. Then it's back down the east coast through the stunning beach areas of Trincomalee and Pasikuda to the ancient capital of Polonnaruwa. Finally you'll stop in Kandy to see the spectacular rock-cave temples of Dambulla, before heading back to Colombo for a breakfast of herbal rice porridge with a famous Colombo chef. Other hungry highlights include a visit to a traditional Jaffna home to watch as Peter makes a delicious Jaffna crab curry; a deep-sea fishing experience with local Trincomalee fishermen; and a lesson in the art of making pittu and the famous egg hoppers that are unique to the eastern coast of Sri Lanka.

....

-O- worldexpeditions.com/Sri-Lanka/Adventure-Touring/
My-Sri-Lanka-with-Peter-Kuruvita

COOKING IN THE YUCATAN, MEXICO

By the end of this culinary adventure, you'll be able to make salsas, guacamole, panuchos, tortillas and then some. So says chef Anita Lo, the culinary lead on Tour de Fork's seven-day Yucatan itinerary. Your Merida base will be an elegant 17th-century hacienda with decadent architecture that includes wide terraces, a library with a well-stocked bar, and beautiful bedrooms with high ceilings. Its stunning gardens encompass walking trails and a swimming pool, the perfect place to relax once you've taken off your apron. In the kitchen, you'll learn the dishes mentioned above along with sopa de tortilla, poc chuc and pollo pibil, the popular cooked-in-the-ground chicken dish. You'll also enjoy food forays into rural Yucatan to explore the beauty of its products and the bounty of its chefs. You'll visit the colourful Merida Market to forage for chickens, fancy fruits, fresh vegetables and corn masa for making tortillas before popping by Merida's Museo de Gastronomia e Restaurante. The itinerary also includes a daytrip to the archaeological site of Uxmal followed by a swim at the incredible cenote (sinkhole) Hacienda Mucuyche and a picnic lunch. The cultural evening at Noche Blanca, an arts festival in Merida's Centro Historico with musicians and street performers, is another highlight.

....

-O- tourdeforks.com/mexico/cooking-in-the-yucatan-with-
chef-anita-lo

FALL INTO FORAGING, SWEDEN

Sweden's wild and rugged Arctic landscape, known as Lapland, is also a forager's paradise where native ingredients flourish. Off the Map Travel's four-night foraging foray begins at Brändön Lodge, a comfortable log-built bolthole nestled in the trees on the coast east of Lulea. From here, a local guide takes you out into the crisp autumnal Arctic air for a lesson in wilderness and survival skills. You'll build a fire using only what you find in nature, examine fresh animal tracks and identify the best place to set up camp (if you ever needed to). With survival skills checked off, it's time to forage for staple ingredients such as lingonberries and cloudberries. The waters along this coastline are similarly filled with some of the Arctic's most prized bounty. On a scenic boat tour you'll fish along the coast then stay overnight at Jopikgården on the secluded island of Hindersön. On the return journey, you'll stop off at a local island to forage for seasonal ingredients including leafy herbs and chanterelle mushrooms. Look out for seals bathing and reindeer wandering. Other highlights include lunch in an authentic Sami tent, where you'll learn more about the indigenous people's traditional way of life. During the trip your produce will be collected and stored in preparation for a cooking class with a specialist Nordic chef who will take you step by step through local techniques and recipes. The culmination of your combined achievements will be a final Arctic dinner — and a deep sense of contentment at having foraged for your own food using wilderness techniques. This micro-level connection to the land is a slow travel essential.

....

-O- offthemap.travel/experiences/otmt-exclusive-fall-into-foraging

On the return journey, you'll stop off at a local island to forage for seasonal ingredients including leafy herbs and chanterelle mushrooms.

SAVOUR JAMES BEARD'S PORTLAND, USA

Portland-born James Beard was known as America's first foodie, a 20th-century cook, author and television personality who championed American cuisine in all its culinary genres. Tour de Forks' four-night itinerary channels the food guru's hometown by teaming up with award-winning food and travel writer Kathleen Squires and Ronnie Rodriguez, famed maître d' of the private dining club Chef's Dinner Series, who together produced the PBS documentary *America's First Foodie: The Incredible Life of James Beard*. Through their contacts you'll meet the chefs and eat at restaurants featured in the documentary. You'll stay at the Heathman Hotel, located in downtown Portland, and use it as a base for exploring the city's foodie scene through the eyes (and stomachs) of Squires and Rodriguez. Highlights include a visit to the award-winning Willamette Valley, a wine region known for its devilishly good pinots and also its craft beer scene – you'll sip on wood-aged, wild and farmhouse styles. On a guided downtown tour you'll taste doughnuts and America's best coffee (it's essential to dunk the doughnut, trust me), and then regroup for a hands-on cooking class and dinner with celeb chef Jenn Louis at her Israeli restaurant, Ray. (You'll also get a copy of her cookbook, *The Book of Greens*, which she co-authored with Squires.) Perhaps the best bit is the Food Cart Tour. You'll board Harry the Van to taste-test the diversity of Portland's food carts, which dish out Persian, Asian, Korean, Thai and Greek food in the form of rice bowls, burritos, wraps, crepes and pizzas.

....

-O- *tourdeforks.com/usa/portland-oregon*

MARKETS, MARSALA AND MARZIPAN: FLAVOURS OF WESTERN SICILY, ITALY

Doing anything in late summer? Just off the toe of Italy's 'boot', Sicily is at the crossroads of the Mediterranean and has drawn many of its cultural and culinary cues from diverse backgrounds. Authentic Adventures' seven-day itinerary, based in Palermo and Marsala, uncovers some of these influences in its introduction to the tastes of sun-drenched Western Sicily. In Palermo, you'll stroll through two markets – the bustling old La Vucciria (which fittingly translates as 'hubbub') and the centuries-old Ballaro with stalls selling olives, cheeses and snacks such as panelle (chickpea fritters). You'll visit the 16th-century Church of San Francesco di Paola where religious art plays second fiddle to the marzipan fruits, or frutta di Martorana, which is made by the monks and given to children on All Souls Day, a Christian feast day. In Marsala, you'll visit Frantoio Centonze, known for its olive groves and grassy green cold-pressed olive oil, and Molini del Ponte flour mill where the ancient grain tumminia is chief ingredient in Pane Nero di Castelvetrano, a sweet, crusty black bread. Still hungry? At the Azienda Cucchiara farm and dairy you'll taste DOP-accredited Pecorino Siciliano cheese made with milk from their own sheep flock, and Vastedda Valle del Belice, a creamy and slightly sour Sicilian 'spun' cheese. Finally you'll pop by Marsala Cellars for a goodbye sip of the town's namesake fortified wine.

....

-O- *authenticadventures.com/tours/gregg-wallace-food-holidays*

SUSHI, SASHIMI, MARKETS AND MORE, JAPAN

Tokyo has the most Michelin-starred restaurants in the world, so it's little wonder that the thought of a sushi and sashimi itinerary might leave you salivating. Abercrombie and Kent's 11-night tour is a deep bow to Japan's culinary legacy in five destinations, staying in high-end luxury hotels along the way. At an Asakusa restaurant in Tokyo you'll sample an array of distinctive battered and deep-fried tempura vegetables before exploring Kappabashi's Kitchen Town and the boisterous and exciting Ameyoko-Cho spice market. With chef Akila Inouye, the founder and president of the Tsukiji Soba Academy, at the helm you'll also master the secrets of making Japanese soba (buckwheat) noodles on a half-day cooking class. In slow-paced Takayama, a preserved old town perched on the forested hillsides of Hida in the Japanese Alps, you'll tour a sake brewery for a lesson on the ancient rice-wine custom before sampling some. You'll also visit the 300-year-old Jinja-mae market to peruse stalls selling vegetables and homemade pickles. Kyoto is another highlight. In the elaborate Nishiki food markets you'll learn about the flavours, ingredients and techniques needed to make rolled sushi, miso soup and cooked salad.

....

-O- abercrombiekent.co.uk/destinations/asia/japan/
sushi-and-sashimi

Tokyo has the most Michelin-starred restaurants in the world.

SHORT ORDER

Immersive cooking experiences don't need to take weeks or even days. Sometimes a few hours or a half-day – a micro food adventure – can land you right in the culinary heart of a destination.

ITALIAN COOKING CLASS, ROME, ITALY

You don't necessarily need a chef to learn the art of cooking saltimbocca alla Romana. One of my most memorable cooking experiences was on Context Travel's half-day Roman cooking class itinerary when I mastered (I think) this recipe with a (good) home cook in the privacy of her own apartment. The experience begins not far from the Colosseum in the city's leafy suburbs with a walk around some typical local shops: a cafe with a gleaming glass counter filled with sfogliateli and cannoli; a deli where oversized salamis and hams dangle from the ceiling; and a pasta shop churning out freshly made rigatoni. Next stop is Testaccio Market, one of Rome's most famous outdoor markets, where you'll pick up some fresh zucchini (courgette) flowers and heritage tomatoes. Then it's home to your host's kitchen to cook a full meal, which will be eaten together at the dining table like old friends.

-O- contexttravel.com

BEEKEEPING EXPERIENCE, TASMANIA, AUSTRALIA

Tasmania's flowering native manuka and fragrant prickly box species are the feeding ground for local bees, resulting in honey with a distinctive flavour profile and strong seasonal variation. On the stunning Freycinet Peninsula, Saffire Freycinet resort's two-hour hive-to-honey experience allows you to get up close and personal to the bees that produce the incredible Wild Hives local honey. In a full-body apiarist suit you'll venture into a nearby private apiary with horticulturalist Rob Barker to witness the adrenaline rush of 60,000 bees per hive, each beating their wings approximately 230 times per second, and experience the breathtaking natural phenomenon of honey-making. From the hive you'll extract warm, fresh honeycomb and taste some of the purest liquid gold on the planet.

-O- saffire-freycinet.com.au/experiences

OYSTER PICKING, ECUADOR

The oysters near the sleepy fishing town of Puerto Cayo, in Ecuador, are reason enough to visit. On Abercrombie and Kent's five-hour oyster picking itinerary you will head out in the sun and salty air on a boat ride to a rocky islet. You'll explore the tide pools and exposed reef at low tide then pluck your own oysters straight from the sea. With an expert chef in tow (and a pop-up dining setting complete with market umbrella) you'll learn how to shuck the oysters with a special knife and then eat them straight-up with that fresh sea-salty flavour, complemented by a glass of chardonnay, obviously.

-O- abercrombiekent.co.uk/destinations/south-america/
    ecuador-and-galapagos-islands/oyster-picking-in-
    ecuador

Right: Preparing oysters in Ecuador
Overleaf: Tasmania's beekeeping experience is a sweet immersion

URBAN SLOW
Calm in big cities

Whether it be an errant itinerary, work, family, pleasure or simple serendipity, slow travellers will occasionally find themselves caught wheeling their luggage through the madness of a big urban metropolis. Don't despair. Far from paradoxical, cities can put to the test the hard-won idea that slow travellers can, at any time, seek out mindful, happy and immersive experiences even when the immediate environment feels time-pressured, polluted, crowded and loud.

Plonk yourself at a cafe and talk to the barista, lie in a park and count the different bird species.

While I grew up in the country and will forever pine for the smell of fresh eucalypt and the freedom of being carried effortlessly downstream by a river current, I have been a city person most of my adult life. When in London in my early twenties, I lived above a shop on a busy street in Highbury. For outdoor action my flatmates and I would climb out a window and sit on the roof to watch the passing clouds. On street level, one of the typical London off-licences, or 'offies', would attract rowdy Arsenal supporters on their way to and from a game. Red double-decker buses – my means of getting to my office job in the city – would screech to a halt right outside the door every 15 minutes. I loved the pace and the chaos and the sensation that life was happening all around me. Back home in Melbourne, I'm still a city-slicker. I live in a warehouse apartment above a cafe in an inner-city hub that ticks all the cosmopolitan boxes – there's a building going up next door, police sirens are standard and the traffic can get tedious. How do I still love it?

On an elemental level, the city offers vignettes of life, community, history and humanity that can be consciously absorbed from the architecture, people, accents, even the street signs. The minutiae we can pick up from the ant-like business of a city and all its facets can be energising. Plonk yourself at a cafe and talk to the barista, lie in a park and count the different bird species. Talk to someone who has been selling ice-cream on the same corner for decades. Then seek out the city's quieter places, those oases of peace where respite comes from the very contrast of transitioning from chaotic to calm. Here are some of the urban oases I've come across while travelling.

Left: Oodi Central Library, Helsinki's new cultural hot spot

Top: Old meets new at Tai Kwun Centre for Heritage and Arts, Hong Kong

Bottom: Word on the Water floating bookshop on Regent's Canal, London

REGENT'S CANAL, LONDON, ENGLAND

In 2020, it will be 200 years since the completion of Regent's Canal in London. Running from the Grand Junction Canal's Paddington Arm to Limehouse near the Thames, the canal was part of a grand plan to have barges in an urban landscape. And for forty years or so it worked. The canal linked to the Grand Junction Canal and the routes running to the Midlands and north, and it carried fuel, building materials, food, liquor and fresh produce in and out of London. When the golden age of the railways arrived, the barge trade – and the horses that dragged them along from the towpath – couldn't keep up. Despite the majority of people living within five miles of a canal or waterway, the railways and lorries dominated. Fast forward to today and the canals enjoy a new life as a wellness opportunity for busy Londoners. According to the Canal and River Trust, the charity that looks after almost 3200 kilometres (2000 miles) of British waterways, research shows that 'spending time by water, whether it be your lunchbreak, daily commute or just a weekend stroll, really does make us feel happier and healthier'. For travellers too, the Regent's Canal provides a more leisurely pace in which to get to know the city. One option is to stroll along the towpath from Granary Square in King's Cross past locks, keepers' cottages and colourful narrow boats north-west towards Camden. Or walk the other way towards Islington past Word on the Water, a floating bookshop, and London Canal Museum.

-O- canalrivertrust.org.uk

KL FOREST ECO PARK, KUALA LUMPUR, MALAYSIA

Few cities can boast a natural rainforest at their heart like Kuala Lumpur. Located a short amble from Kuala Lumpur Menara Tower, KL Forest Eco Park (formerly known as the Bukit Nanas Forest Reserve or Pineapple Hill) was gazetted in 1906, which makes it one of the oldest permanent forest reserves in Malaysia. While the din of distant traffic can still be heard in some parts, and the city's high-rise apartment buildings peep through the trees like metropolis mega-fauna, the city is easily left behind in a forest alive with tropical plants, snaking vines, century-old hardwood trees, ferns and a dappled emerald-green tree canopy. On the concrete paths and staircases you leave behind the urban jungle for a real jungle with a symphony of singing crickets, buzzing insects, nattering monkeys, squeaking birds and rustling branches. To get some height on the Kuala Lumpur skyline, enter the park via the tower carpark and follow signposts to the Canopy Walk, a 200-metre-high (656-foot-high) and slightly wobbly series of adjoining wood-and-steel bridges, accessed via spiral staircases. If heights aren't your thing, enter via Jalan Raja Chulan where the information centre has other trail maps. This is one to do before the heat and humidity of the day kick in.

-O- menarakl.com.my/index.php/attractions/tower-attractions/kl-forest-eco-park

Spanning four city blocks and hosting 7.5 million visitors each year, the Metropolitan Museum of Art, fondly known as the Met, is a New York art-lovers heavyweight. There are three branches including the Met Cloisters and the Met Breuer but it is the Met Fifth Avenue that has the space (185,806 square metres or 2 million square feet), the history (5000 years of art) and the architecture (a five-storey Neoclassical wonder) to lose yourself in. And you will lose yourself. The 2-million-piece collection of global art and artefacts is too immense to try to get around; it's better to choose a subject in a small quiet corner and engross yourself in it. Highlights include the American Wing with its US Bank facade and courtyard of sculptures; the European Paintings wing with works by Botticelli, Caravaggio, Rembrandt, Monet and Degas (the list goes on); and the Asian Art wing where an inner courtyard, the Astor Chinese Garden Court (the first of its kind built outside China in 1981), offers peaceful respite. From May to October, the fifth-floor rooftop garden and cafe is a hidey-hole of calm with a treetop view across Central Park to the Manhattan skyline. And if the thought of other people drives you to distraction, join a private guided Empty Met Tour to explore this incredible place when it is closed to the public.

METROPOLITAN MUSEUM OF ART, NEW YORK, USA

-O- *metmuseum.org*

TAI KWUN CENTRE FOR HERITAGE AND ARTS, HONG KONG

An entire unused block on Hollywood Road in the dense urban-heart of Hong Kong Central has, after a decade, opened as Tai Kwun Centre for Heritage and Arts. Surrounded by old colonial masonry walls of what was the justice compound, the 13,600-square-metre (146,389-square-foot) space includes 16 repurposed historic buildings and two new edifices. Costing HK$3.8 billion (US$484 million) the revitalisation project has transformed a derelict heritage site into a world-class public space, a low-rise oasis in a city of high-rises. The site's mix of open spaces, laneways and multi-storey architecture ensures there are plenty of nooks and crannies to get lost in. There's a prominent Parade Ground where you can sit under the shade of a 60-year-old mango tree, a red brick former Police Headquarters housing major exhibitions and multi-use performance spaces, and the grandiose four-storey Barrack Block with bookshops and boutiques. The former Superintendent's House and old Ablution Block have been renovated and repurposed as theatre, gallery and studio spaces where during off-peak times it's possible to be the only spectator. At the southern end of the compound two spectacular new multi-storey builds – JC Cube performance venue and JC Contemporary exhibition space – produce and host world-class dance, art, performance and music from a uniquely Hong Kong perspective. Kick around in the former Prison Yard, a courtyard communal space with art installations, shops and cafes, and look out for free weekend feature films.

....

-O- taikwun.hk/en

ABBOTSFORD CONVENT, MELBOURNE, AUSTRALIA

On the traditional lands of the Wurundjeri people in a natural amphitheatre on the banks of the Yarra River, heritage-listed Abbotsford Convent is a religious institution turned urban retreat for inner Melbourne. Its restored buildings have become the creative hub for more than 100 artists, writers, artisans and wellness practitioners, and the heirloom gardens that once surrounded Victorian-era rural mansions are now a pleasure place for walkers, daydreamers and butterfly chasers. Revolving exhibitions, art installations, talks and workshops are held each week and on weekends the place is abuzz with farmers' markets, book stalls and acoustic tunes. A dirt path passes under fig trees down to the river, where it reaches the paved Yarra walking and cycle trail. This 33-kilometre (20.5-mile) love-in for anyone on two wheels or two feet navigates past waterfalls, over bridges and alongside picnic spots on a restorative waterside meander from Eltham all the way to the city. Next door to the convent, the Collingwood Children's Farm is another attraction prized for its slow relief. It's a wholesomely rural plot with hay bales and corrugated-iron sheds where you can milk a cow, hold a guinea pig, wander among the pigs and goats or sit under the shade of a gum by the river. Enjoy outdoor eating options at both the convent and the farm along with plenty of grassy spots perfectly suited to a picnic rug.

-O- *abbotsfordconvent.com.au*

OODI CENTRAL LIBRARY, HELSINKI, FINLAND

Described as an ode to 'Finnish culture, equality and freedom of expression', Helsinki's new € 98 million library opened in December 2018 to celebrate the country's 101 years of independence. Perish the thought of a dowdy council building with musty books, this contemporary urban space, at Kansalaistori Square in the heart of the city, is an architectural marvel that transcends previous notions of what a library should be. Dubbed a 'civic living room' Oodi combines literature with urban experiences aimed to attract a diverse crowd. For visitors to the city it's an eye on the local community as much as it is a tranquil place for more contemplative endeavours. Its three floors have distinct atmospheres. The first floor is a busy coming-and-going space with lobby events, book returns, a cafe and a cinema with screenings in languages including English. The second floor is a work hub with tiered seating for meet-ups, workshop rooms and state-of-the-art studio space where creatives have access to trade tools including recording, filming and editing equipment as well as 3D scanners, laser cutters and sewing machines. The third floor, with the library, fuses the mood of a good bookshop (there are 100,000 items to borrow) with inventive breakout spaces for reading and playing board games. Armchairs have window views so you can kick back and watch the weather. There's a cafe on this level along with the Citizens Balcony, which overlooks Parliament House and the Töölönlahti Park. There are also nine living trees that reach for the ceiling.

-O- *oodihelsinki.fi/en*

INTO THE DARK

A city by night can feel like the distant relative of the same city by day because the visual, social and sensual landscapes change dramatically. Nocturnal adventures can expose these changes – heightening the senses and igniting the imagination so that travellers see the environment in a different light. The wilderness can be equally appealing at night for its inky darkness … for it is in the blackest of nights that the stars shine brightest.

GLOW ART FESTIVAL, EINDHOVEN, NETHERLANDS

The city of Eindhoven has light in its DNA. The match industry was established here in 1870 and Philips opened an incandescent light bulb factory here in 1891. The GLOW light art festival, held over a week in November each year, sees the city's facades, trees, pathways and public spaces re-imagined by unusual and creative light projections and installations. The fascinating works are created by more than 30 national and international light artists who work on a different theme each year. In 2015 the theme was Nature and Architecture, in 2019 it was Living Colours. The vision is spectacular, attracting hundreds of thousands of visitors who follow a walking route connecting the artworks. Despite the crowds, the walk is an ethereal immersion best taken slowly and mindfully.

-O- gloweindhoven.nl/en

FLUO NIGHT DIVING, MALDIVES

By day blue-green waters lap at white-sand shores, by night neon-lit corals and a rainbow of fish light up the dark watery underworld. The Baros resort in the Maldives opened the first dive centre in the archipelago in 1979. The Fluo Night Dive is one of the more daring dives allowing guests to see the reef in an entirely different light. It's completely safe for certified divers due to the resort's close proximity to the sheltered waters on the house reef. Accompanied by an instructor fully qualified to lead night dives, you will dive with a yellow barrier filter over your mask plus lights specifically designed to generate the maximum amount of bio-fluorescence (or blue light). Some corals and marine life absorb part of the blue light and in return emit unusual yellows, greens, pinks and blues. The fluorescence effect is exquisite.

-O- baros.com

REDWOODS NIGHTLIGHTS, ROTORUA, NEW ZEALAND

Rotorua's California Redwoods forest, planted in the early 1900s, lies within the Whakarewarewa Forest, one of the oldest exotic nature-scapes in New Zealand. The Redwoods Treewalk, a 700-metre-long (2297-foot-long) eco-tourism experience on elevated walkways, takes you up as high as 20 metres (65 feet) among the trees and captures the peace, ambience and spirit of this natural beauty. Visiting it after dark is another experience again. On a Redwoods Nightlights walk you'll immerse yourself in an arboreal wonderland, with the redwoods, forest ferns and pungas illuminated by designer David Trubridge's 40 colour spotlights and 30 bespoke lanterns. These magical two-metre (6.5-foot) lights permeate the darkness with an other-worldly glow.

-O- treewalk.co.nz/en_US

Right: New Zealand's Redwoods Nightlights

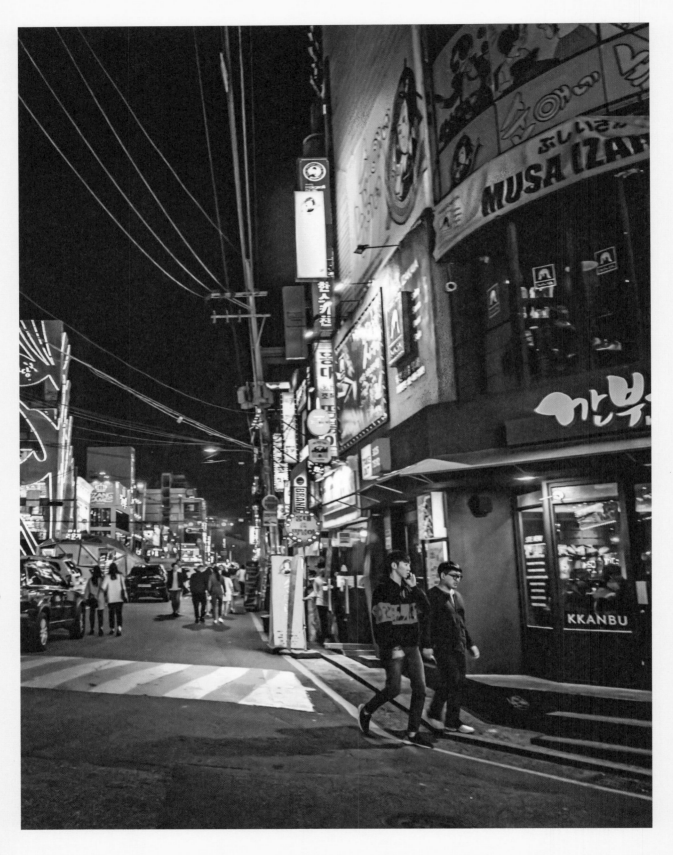

DARK SKY SANCTUARY, RAKIURA, NEW ZEALAND

Stewart Island's Māori name, Rakiura – loosely translated as 'land of the glowing skies' – is more fitting than ever given the island, New Zealand's third largest, has been recognised as an international Dark Sky Sanctuary for its exceptionally clear night skies. It is the fifth official Dark Sky Sanctuary in the world, and only the second island sanctuary (the first is also in New Zealand). Rakiura is located off the bottom of the South Island, at 46 degrees south and 168 degrees east; there are few landmasses that share this special outlook, which provides some of the best views of the aurora australis (southern lights). You can see the lights best when immersed in the native bush and rugged coastlines of Rakiura National Park, or on the multi-day Rakiura Track, one of the country's great walks.

....

-O- stewartisland.co.nz

CHELATNA LAKE LODGE, ALASKA

At the other end of the planet, Chelatna Lake Lodge, just south of Alaska's ice-peaked Denali National Park, offers another resplendent night-time vantage point. From here guests at this dark-sky lodge can watch as the northern lights – the aurora borealis – colour the sky in an ethereal wash of green, blue and pink. The fly-in lodge, with cedar-lined chalets, is miles from any road system and a long way from any metropolis so light pollution is virtually zero. You can end the day watching the lights in the sky from the cosy glassed-in living room or outside in the steaming lakeside cedar hot tub. The lights peak in March so time your run.

....

-O- chelatna.com

SEOUL NIGHT TOUR, SOUTH KOREA

The countercultural and youthful heart of Seoul is under the lens on Context Travel's three-hour Seoul Night Tour through the Hongdae and Yeonnam-dong neighbourhoods. As the sun goes down, you'll join a Korean cultural expert on an exploration of traditional life, pop culture, contemporary design and cuisine. In Yeonnam-dong you'll see that old-school charm mixes it up with hip streets and alleyways. You'll navigate past vintage shops and street art and stop by Dongin Market, where young makers sell their on-trend crafts and handmade items. In Hongdae you might visit a quirky animal-themed cafe and a local film set before getting an intro to K-Indie. This music, produced by independent record labels, has flourished in the area's divey venues that are loved by local musos. Finish the tour with a delicious Korean barbecue.

....

-O- contexttravel.com/cities/seoul/tours/seoul-night-tour-
    in-hip-hongdae

Left: Seoul Night Tour through Hongdae

Slow traveller and microadventurer

Alastair Humphreys is a British adventurer, an author of ten books about his travels and a keynote speaker. His many global expeditions include a 74,000-kilometre (46,000-mile), four-year cycle trip around the world, a 966-kilometre (600-mile) coast-to-coast walk across India and a 4700-kilometre (2920-mile) rowing adventure across the Atlantic. He's also known as a microadventurer, a pioneering term that Humphreys, through a litany of backyard UK immersions, almost coined himself. His pioneering work on the concept saw him named National Geographic Adventurer of the Year in 2012.

INTERVIEW:

ALASTAIR HUMPHREYS

Microadventures are adventures that are 'short, simple, local, cheap – yet still fun, exciting, challenging, refreshing and rewarding', according to Humphreys. As the world becomes increasingly prone to indoor lifestyles, digitised spaces and urbanised environs, microadventures offer 'a realistic escape to wilderness, simplicity and the great outdoors, without the need to ski to the South Pole or go live in a cabin in Patagonia'. They fit neatly into the slow travel space as many of Humphreys' adventures show. (As an aside, Humphreys is also single-handedly responsible for inspiring my partner to disappear along Melbourne's Yarra River with my two kids and a swag for a night every now and then. I get 17 hours of me-time every time that happens. Kudos.)

Favourite slow adventures?

As you can see from my blog (alastairhumphreys.com) I've had some good slow adventures. I went to Scotland to cram a week full of three of the things I love most in life: ride my mountain bike, play with my camera and sleep in bothies. A bothy is a simple shelter, in remote country, for the use and benefit of all who love wild and lonely places. Bothies are left unlocked and are available for anyone to use free of charge. The shelters are rudimentary and basic, but when the weather is howling – those times when you think 'this is miserable, but the misery does mean something' – a night in a bothy might be all you need from life.

I also spent five days rafting down the Klarälven River in Sweden. It took a few hours, plenty of clove hitches, and several hundred metres of rope to turn a pile of logs into a beautiful raft, sturdy enough for six of us. Pushing off from the bank and out into the current was a magical feeling. We settled down to the slowest adventure of our lives … At the beginning we were all in 'work mode' – our minds whirring, needing to be busy, wondering always what to do next, chattering, fidgeting. It takes time to slow down, to remember how to sit still, to be quiet, to enjoy the view right here rather than impatiently wondering what it will be like round the next corner.

What style of microadventure would you recommend to someone who wants to start travelling and seeing the world in a slower, more insightful way?

I think the key is to not overthink, but to act. Not to plan a year-long slow journey and sell your house, but rather to go sleep on your hill for one night, then return home slightly changed. Also, nothing beats travelling by bicycle! A motorbike may be faster; walking may be slower (there is a time and a place for both fast adventure and slow adventure). Kayaks and canoes and crampons may get you to wilder places. Living and working in a foreign land may engage you deeper into a culture. But a journey by bike does a pretty good job at every one of these aspects.

Where or what is your next slow adventure?

I don't know, to be honest! But I am making an effort this year to climb the same tree once a month. I have a calendar reminder, the tree is close to my home, and simply taking 30 minutes to go there on a monthly basis is a really, really good way to refocus, evaluate, reflect and pay attention to the changing seasons. The same things I loved when I did four seasons of microadventures in one year. Basically, once a season I spent a night out in the same woods. It's a simple idea: a way to see how the world changes, to measure my own year and make plans, and to experience the outdoors in a variety of ways.

Overleaf: JC Cube Museum in Tai Kwun Centre for Heritage Arts, Hong Kong is the perfect example of urban slow (see p. 156)

TRAILS LESS TRAVELLED

New walks, parks and preserves in nature

While it might feel like we have the world mapped out in terms of hiking trails, national parks and natural wonders, there are in fact new and inspiring routes and destinations unveiled on a regular basis. For slow travellers this is an opportunity to explore trails less travelled in far corners of the planet (hopefully before the crowds get there). The opening of the Ruta de Los Parques in Chile and Canada's Great Trail unleashed thousands of kilometres of relatively uncharted terrain into public hands. Costa Rica's Poás Volcano National Park provides an intrepid opportunity to witness a geothermal wonder in safe proximity. The best of these newly opened attractions help to sustain the local communities. They also have uplifting back-stories about their sustainability and contribution to the future of the planet. These aspects enable travellers to maximise their positive impact.

The best of these newly opened attractions help to sustain the local communities.

Top: Canada's Great Trail

Right top: Cerro Castillo National Park in Chilean Patagonia

Right bottom: Jenner Headlands Preserve, California

The Poás Volcano doesn't spew lava or erupt, but every so often it shoots millions of tonnes of ash, steam, smoke and rock into the air. One of the latest incidents, in April 2017, induced the government to close the national park, but it has since reopened with new security measures including poison gas monitors, concrete bunkers and emergency filters. Don't let all this turn you off – the power of Costa Rica's geothermal underworld is on show again and it's worth a visit. The park is in the province of Alajuela, 48 kilometres (30 miles) north of the capital city of San José. Poás, the main volcano tipping 2700 metres (8900 feet), is one of the country's six active volcanos. You can buy tickets, which include guided walks through the intriguing geography that feels like a lunar landscape. The effects of acid rain are evident in the stunted brown and black vegetation tainted by the moisture from the omnipresent clouds near the peak. You can walk close to the Poás summit, where the crater – 320 metres (1050 feet) deep and 1.6 kilometres (1 mile) in diameter (the largest active crater in the world) – cups a sulphuric, bubbling, turquoise rain-fed lake. The lake produces steam geysers that rocket 250 metres (820 feet) into the air but, fear not, spectators are well out of the way. There's a paved walk to the viewing platform and a short Escalonia cloud-forest trail where you're a chance to spot hummingbirds and two of the endemic species: Poás squirrels and the pagoda-shaped escalonia trees.

POÁS VOLCANO NATIONAL PARK, COSTA RICA

....

-O- costa-rica-guide.com/nature/national-parks/
poas-volcano

RUTA DE LOS PARQUES, CHILE

In April 2019 Tompkins Conservation officially handed over more than 4070 square kilometres (1570 square miles) of privately owned and fastidiously conserved land to the Chilean Government. The Chilean Government also contributed over 10,000 square kilometres (almost 4000 square miles) and reclassified almost 22,000 square kilometres (8500 square miles) of nature reserves as national parks. These unprecedented contributions formed the creation of five new national parks (Pumalín Douglas Tompkins, Melimoyu, Cerro Castillo, Patagonia and Kawésqar) and the expansion of three others (Hornopirén, Corcovado and Isla Magdalena).Together these parks, along with nine others, form the truly awe-inspiring Ruta de Los Parques, or Route of Parks of Chilean Patagonia. Over three regions, the land is more than twice as big as Costa Rica and three times the size of Switzerland. Ninety-one per cent of the land is protected national park territory. You can explore it along a 2800-kilometre (1700-mile) scenic route spanning the 17 national parks between Puerto Montt and Cape Horn in Chile's far south. The route connects the northern Carretera Austral, which winds its way along Chilean Patagonia, with the central Patagonian Channels and the southern Ruta del Fin del Mundo (the End of the World Route). The route is pristine and diverse, revealing lakes, glaciers, rainforests, cloud-covered valleys and 60 local communities. Take it and you'll experience nature, cultural immersion, solitude and physical activity – elements at the heart of slow travel.

-O- rutadelosparques.org

JENNER HEADLANDS PRESERVE, USA

California's coastal old-growth forests once covered thousands of square kilometres along the Sonoma coast. Logging over the past 150 years has reduced these forests by more than 95 per cent. Covering 23 square kilometres (9 square miles), the new Jenner Headlands Preserve, near Jenner in Sonoma County, California, is an antidote to the destruction. It aims to nurture the re-growth of these large, mature conifer and hardwood trees and conserve and improve habitat for rare, threatened and endangered species. It's a project of California's Wildlands Conservancy, which for 20 years has rescued important landscapes from development to create the state's largest nature preserve system. You can appreciate these efforts exploring the preserve's 23 kilometres (14 miles) of trails that undulate in and out of dazzling Pacific Coast views. Many of the trails pass through towering redwood and Douglas fir forests inhabited by species including the northern spotted owl, peregrine falcon, deer and coyote. The preserve has been designed to appeal to all ages and abilities with diverse walks including the short paved Hawk Hill trail to a scenic viewpoint and the more rugged 24-kilometre (15-mile) Sea to Sky hike from sea level to the top of Pole Mountain, which at 672 metres (2204 feet) is the highest point on the Sonoma Coast. It's open from 8am until the sun sets over that pounding blue ocean.

-O- wildlandsconservancy.org/preserve_jenner.html

THE GREAT TRAIL, CANADA

Twenty-five years is a long time spent on any project but the hours put into creating Canada's Great Trail, spanning 13 provinces and territories, will be well matched with the accumulated hours that walkers, skiers, hikers, canoeists and nature lovers spend on it in the years to come. Completed in 2017, this is the world's longest recreational trail, stretching more than 24,000 kilometres (15,000 miles) coast to coast across the country, with a northern loop through the Arctic. It links 15,000 communities – a conduit for people, ideas and cultures – and traverses 'the wild, the rural and the urban by waterways, roadways and footpaths'. There are plenty of ways to explore it. On Vancouver Island you can have a self-guided adventure exploring British Columbia's west coast on the island-hopping Salish Sea Marine Trail. In Ontario, the Lake Superior Water Trail passes Canada's largest freshwater lake. On the rocks along the shoreline, Agawa Rock Pictographs – paintings of canoes, moose, deer, bear and caribou dating back to the 16th century – are evidence of the history of many Ojibwe indigenous communities. The back-country Itijjagiaq Trail, in Nunavut, crosses Baffin Island where Inuit populations lived for generations. It remains a popular location for fishing Arctic char, picking berries, hunting geese and admiring the expansive Arctic vistas.

....

-O- *thegreattrail.ca*

OLD GHOST ROAD, NEW ZEALAND

Trampers (as you're called in New Zealand), lace your boots; mountain-bikers, saddle up. In the north-west corner of New Zealand's South Island a remote and wild old gold-miners' road, built in the 1870s, has been revived as a multi-day mountain-biking and hiking trail. Dubbed an outdoor museum by its founders, the 85-kilomentre (53-mile) Old Ghost Road connects the old dray road in the ghost town of Lyell to Seddonville and the mighty Mokihinui River in the north. On the way you'll traverse narrow winding trails through native forests, river flats and gorges, over picturesque bridges and along magical mountain-top ridges. Adding intrigue and storytelling to the adventure, the trail route has four eerily abandoned ghost towns where miners put tools down long ago. Experienced bikers and back-country trampers can traverse the entire trail over two (bikers) and five (trampers) days, or on shorter overnight return trips and daytrips accessed at the trail heads. Accommodation is in characteristic wooden huts, set in spectacular locations where starry nights and sunsets are part of the experience. The favourites have bunk beds with mattresses, cooking facilities, composting toilets, wood fires and quirky showers. In the warmer months, sleep-outs and tent options give you the chance to really go wild. The south–north journey ends in Seddonville where the only business in town is a pub – a worthy place for a beer.

....

-O- *oldghostroad.org.nz*

FOOTPRINTS

Travelling slow means travelling sustainably. Over-tourism has come to be seen as the antithesis of slow and sustainable travel. The unprecedented numbers of tourists in hot spots such as Paris, Venice, Barcelona, Santorini, Dubrovnik and Bangkok has angered locals, who rightly claim mass tourism threatens the very nature of the destination. Raucous behaviour has also raised eyebrows. Kyoto residents have decried half-naked hikers, long lenses pointed in the face of geisha residents and dive-bombing in onsens, while in Amsterdam rowdy cruise-ship visitors and tourists on boozy boat and beer bike rides have made the city almost unliveable for residents. The over-tourism backlash has been global. Dubrovnik has put a limit on cruise-ship numbers and Venice has re-routed the larger vessels away from its Grand Canal. Amsterdam has banned short-term Airbnb rentals and stopped these 'fun rides'. Barcelona is planning new tourism taxes while Italian tourist favourites Rome and Cinque Terre are preparing to limit tourist numbers.

Softer measures have also come into play. Kyoto Convention and Visitors Bureau has released an etiquette guide that includes requests for tourists to remove their shoes before stepping on tatami and to refrain from touching old buildings and objects. Ever ahead of the game, New Zealand Tourism has launched the Tiaki Promise (https://tiakinewzealand.com), a beautifully poetic pledge for visitors to Aotearoa, which says:

While travelling in New Zealand I will
Care for land, sea and nature, treading lightly
and leaving no trace
Travel safely, showing care and consideration for all
Respect culture, travelling with an open heart
and mind

As a slow traveller, this feels like the right kind of mantra – to actively seek out experiences and destinations that maintain respect for the locale and help preserve people and place. Whether we're booking flights and accommodation or choosing tours and experiences, there are ways and means of treading more lightly … if at all.

CARDAMOM TENTED CAMP, CAMBODIA

Illegal logging, poaching and habitat destruction are some of the issues that plague Cambodia's natural resources, so it's positive to see the tourism industry helping to combat the problem. Cardamom Tented Camp, on an 180-square-kilometre (70-square-mile) concession in Botum Sakor National Park in western Cambodia's Koh Kong Province, is an eco-camp with nine comfortable safari-style tents set on raised platforms and accessed via boardwalks to help minimise the human footprint. The camp infrastructure has been built with natural building materials and is solar-powered with wastewater and waste-management systems in place. Since opening in 2017, the camp has integrated the role of 12 forest rangers into the guest experience, an initiative that saw it nominated as one of the finalists in the World Travel and Tourism Council's Changemakers Award category, which focuses on fighting illegal wildlife trade through sustainable tourism. The camp also mounted 40 camera traps in strategic locations across the park to keep tabs on 'vulnerable' or 'endangered' species such as the beautiful clouded leopard, sun bear, greater hog badger and now critically endangered Sunda pangolin. You can sign up for two new conservation tourism initiatives: a four-night wildlife release 'Adventurer' including a visit to the Wildlife Alliance's Wildlife Release Station in Chi Phat, and a three-day 'Jungle Camp' using Tentsile tree-tents pitched along abandoned poaching and logging trails.

-O- cardamomtentedcamp.com

BEDANDTREE.COM, GLOBAL

Also called B'n'Tree, a play on B'n'B, this heartfelt online start-up is the tree-hugging idea of German global nomad Chris Kaiser, who has harnessed a way to make long-term travel more sustainable. For every booking originating on Bedandtree with partners including Booking.com, Expedia, Agoda, TripAdvisor and Skyscanner, Chris and his team plant at least one tree – at no cost to the traveller. The idea took hold in 2012: Kaiser was based in Southern Thailand and witnessed the dramatic effects of deforestation. With increasing population and a booming tourism industry, forests in Thailand have been reduced within a century from 80 per cent coverage to only 22 per cent, which meant, crucially, a decreased loss of habitat for critically endangered Asian elephants, Malayan tapirs, Sumatran tigers and Malayan sun bears. Kaiser's love of elephants in particular nurtured the idea that planting trees would help fight climate change, create habitat for wildlife and generate jobs for local communities. That it could be funded by the very overseas travel operators and booking platforms that bring tourists to Thailand was the clincher. By early 2019, Bedandtree had planted more than 50,000 trees, with numbers doubling month on month. The main tree-planting site is in Madagascar where 13,862 mangrove trees have been planted as of January 2019. To plant a tree next time you travel, head to the website and click through to the booking platform.

-O- bedandtree.com

ARKABA CONSERVANCY, AUSTRALIA

Wilpena Pound, in South Australia's Ikara–Flinders Ranges National Park, is a huge geological crater-like amphitheatre, one of the country's most ancient and ecologically significant landscapes. On its edge sits Arkaba Conservancy, a sheep farm turned private bush wilderness. It hosts just ten guests in five luxury rooms located in the old Arkaba Homestead. Arkaba's guiding philosophy is a commitment to conserving Australia's natural habitat. For the past ten years, the conservation team has worked to protect the native species and environment by actively controlling feral cats, foxes and other feral predators using a combination of techniques including traps, baiting and collars. Since their efforts began, reports suggest a dramatic increase in native mammal, bird and reptile populations. Home to one of Australian Wildlife Journeys' nature experiences, the lucky few can go on bush safari and revel in the craggy sandstone bluffs and dry creek beds of this prehistoric landscape or take cover in the animal hide, from where you can watch the native creatures unnoticed. You'll see bird species, including the common bronzewing, Australasian pipit, Australian owlet-nightjar and short-tailed grass wren. So far, Arkaba has changed the lives of 5,457,465 native animals … and counting.

-O- australianwildlifejourneys.com

Left: Jungle kayaking, Cardamom Tented Camp, Cambodia

Overleaf: New Zealand's Old Ghost Road (see p. 171)

UNPLUGGED

Digital detox and off-grid destinations

It doesn't matter which survey or research study you read, the stats are sobering. The average person spends oodles of time on their screen, checks their phone too many times a day and finds it difficult to ignore pings, beeps and buzzes, even when it negatively affects the rest of their life. Two-thirds of the world's population have a mobile phone and, as you're reading this, four billion people around the world are currently using the internet. As groundbreakingly connective as it is, the digital world is taking its toll on how we connect on a micro-level with the world – and people – around us.

There are many digital detox destinations and unplugged places in this book (revisit the Go Beyond (*see* p. 72) and Staying Afloat (*see* p. 84) chapters for starters). If these destinations alone aren't enough to whet your appetite for downtime, the following off-grid specialists can help you turn off the screen and power up your mind.

Top: Kagga Kamma in South Africa, where Host Unusual offers a getaway

Right top: Much Better Adventure's Sahara desert trek

Right bottom: Unyoked's wild cabins within two hours of Sydney and Melbourne

HOST UNUSUAL, GLOBAL

Host Unusual is a website dedicated to quirky, curious and quaint getaways mostly in the UK and Europe, but beyond as well. The style of accommodation ranges from 'castles and follies' and 'caves and grottoes' to 'tiny houses', 'towers and forts' and 'treehouses'. If you feel the need to completely disconnect, the site has an off-grid category with locations deliberately unconnected to electricity and other mainstream power sources, 'allowing you to flick your holiday off switch'. Reams of options are available. There's an architect-designed 'Arctic Hideaway', a cluster of houses on the remote Norwegian island of Fleinvær. Four of the houses are dedicated to sleep, one to preparing and cooking food, a studio living house, a bathhouse and an invigorating sauna. The final house, raised on its own pillar, is dedicated simply to 'contemplating the beauty of life and finding your own inspiration'. On the western cape of South Africa Kagga Kamma is another option. It's a nature resort literally built into the arid rocky landscape of the Cederberg Mountains. From your open-air suite or authentic thatched hut eyrie you'll look upon a wild landscape of birds, aardvarks and zebras, and rock formations featuring ancient art. With no television, wifi or mobile reception, you'll have plenty of time for an outdoor shower and open-air spa bath.

-O- hostunusual.com

UNYOKED, AUSTRALIA

'Minimum footprint, maximum chill' is one of the catchlines coined by Unyoked to promote their designer wilderness cabins hidden in secret locations within two hours of either Melbourne or Sydney. The six cabins all have neat little interiors with throw-cushioned double-beds, mini-kitchens and bathrooms with classy brass fittings. Chilli ratings hint at how deep into the wilderness you'll be. The three-chilli spicy rating involves a 'short trek through the woods, up a hill or a jungle path ... with middle of nowhere vibes'. The two-chilli mild rating is 'still epic wilderness and adventure ... but close enough to know someone's there juuust in case'. Tellingly there's no one-chilli rating because that would be lame. 'Miguel' (all the cabins are named after presumably fictional travelling characters) is a little black timber cabin in the Southern Highlands south of Sydney. It's tucked away in a secluded spot in a 400-year-old rainforest and is accessed via a short walk through the trees. 'It's about as close to nature as you can get ... unless you're actually a tree,' says Unyoked. The cabin has essentials such as a picnic table, fire pit, composting toilet, hot shower, solar power, gas stove and bar fridge, plus some little extras to suit the modern inner-urbanite – from 'awesome coffee' and organic hand-wash to a supply of board games, yoga mats and books.

-O- unyoked.co

Top and right: Host Unusual's Arctic Hideaway, Norway

Bottom: One of Unyoked's cabins tucked away in the Australian bush

OFF THE GRID TRAVEL, AUSTRALIA AND THE SOUTH PACIFIC

You'll spend your time exploring 'iridescent seas, jade jungles and crystal waterfalls' in three waterside destinations.

It's a slow travel conundrum: you want to get off-grid but it's difficult to find and book accommodation if the venue is genuinely unplugged. But it can be done. Off the Grid Travel's line-up of Antipodean destinations gets you to far-off places where there's little chance of your phone pinging. To help your digital detox, the itineraries have off-grid ratings, starting at one – 'Phone service (mostly), internet (mostly), TV if you like, hot showers, modern toilets, shops' – to four – 'Phone useless, internet a memory, loo not guaranteed (trees available), no electricity, bathe in a stream'. Destinations include Aitutaki in the Cook Islands, Freycinet National Park in Australia's island state of Tasmania, and Samoa, a Polynesian island nation in the South Pacific between New Zealand and Hawaii. This latter seven-night self-drive itinerary circumnavigating the island of Upolu is rated two ('Phone service patchy, internet patchier, TV signal scarce, occasional long drops, shops few'). You'll spend your time exploring 'iridescent seas, jade jungles and crystal waterfalls' in three waterside destinations. The highlight is a night in a traditional Samoan beach fale, an open-sided waterfront beach hut with a mattress on the floor and a mosquito net. The days are yours to kayak, snorkel, swim and luxuriate in the natural world without disruption.

Top: A tropical getaway on Upolu Island, Samoa, with Off the Grid Travel

Right: Starlit Moroccan skies

 offthegridtravel.com.au

MUCH BETTER ADVENTURES, GLOBAL

Styled for people 'with zero to 21 days off work', this British outdoor adventure company is focused on helping active people go off-grid for a quick weekend or longer in wild places around the globe. The trip categories include 'epic weekends', 'kayak journeys' and 'summit fever' and all combine challenges and activities with downtime among the desert, rocks, rivers or whatever wild environment you're exploring. According to co-founder Sam Bruce the company likes to keep costs down, 'so we can do more adventures. That means we usually camp, stay in mountain refuges or friendly local guesthouses. Occasionally we'll splash out on a treat'. Bruce believes adventures are for everyone, not just bearded mountaineers, so they make sure there is always a wide range of options to suit all tastes. Itineraries include a three-night sea kayak in Sardinia's Porto Conte Regional Park with its 60 kilometres (37 miles) of protected coastline. You'll explore archaeological sites, churches, ancient fortifications, beaches, bays and parks. If you're after a high you can take three days in Morocco to conquer Mount Toubkal (4167 metres; 13,671 feet), North Africa's highest peak, then camel trek to a traditional Berber camp to sleep in Morocco's Sahara desert. There's also a nine-day Sun Kosi rafting expedition in Nepal. From the Tibetan border you'll journey 270 kilometres (168 miles) on warm waters and rapids, past white sandy beaches, jungles and temples to the Ganges and the flat plains near the Indian border. Local guides organise all the logistics, and one per cent of trip revenue goes to protecting the world's wild places.

-O- *muchbetteradventures.com*

Urban rewilder

INTERVIEW:

CLAIRE DUNN

Restoring eco-systems to their natural state so they can once again sustain themselves is a global movement that sheds light on the often despairing state of the planet. It's called 'rewilding' and it refers not only to the reintroduction of native plants, trees and vegetation to once-bountiful landscapes, but also to the rehabilitation of wildlife in its natural environment. An extension of this rewilding trend is 'urban rewilding', which focuses not on plants and animals but on humans and their innate need to find a place within nature despite living in built-up environments.

Australian rewilder, writer, author and barefoot explorer Claire Dunn once spent a year rewilding in the wilderness – eating bush food, building natural shelters and tanning hides for clothes. She wrote about her experiences in a memoir, My Year Without Matches. More recently she's focusing on urban rewilding. From her hometown of Melbourne, she now runs Rewild Fridays (find more at naturesapprentice.com.au), which are urban dives 'into deep connection practices between humans and nature' through learning bush skills such as bird language, foraging for wild edibles and medicinals, fire making and shelter building. In her forthcoming book, Rewilding the Urban Soul, Dunn goes deeper on the subject. I spoke with her to discover more.

What is urban rewilding and why is it gaining in popularity?
The old ways are new again for the many now seeking to (re)learn the skills, practices and mindsets of our ancestors – everything from food to footwear. It's a movement that's become known as 'rewilding': a return to a wilder or more natural way of being; a process of undoing, un-domestication and connecting with nature.

Suddenly everyone seems to be doing it – following Paleo and 5 by 2 diets, donning barefoot shoes, getting handy with a bow and arrow. Facebook groups dedicated to traditional skills, foraging, natural movement, wild edibles, nature connection and bushcraft are thriving.

One Huffington Post pundit predicts rewilding to be the next big human movement, a kind of post-environmentalism. In contrast to the 'back to the land' movement of the 1970s, rewilding is as much urban as it is rural – wildness rather than wilderness – and philosophical as much as practical. In a historical tipping point, now more than half the world's population live in urban areas. It's imperative that we cultivate a sense of connectivity and belonging in the urban areas we live in. At its core, urban rewilding is about connectivity – to the Earth, to each other and to our own wild nature.

Is it really possible to rewild while living in the city? What are some of the basics?

The practices and projects of urban rewilding are many and varied. One of the most powerful doorways for me is my 'sit spot' – a place in my backyard down in a wild area by the river where I go as often as I can and soak in the life around me. A sit spot in a wildish area within 5 minutes' walk from your home is an efficient way to step out of the human-dominated landscape and into relationship with the more-than-human world. Imagine your neighbourhood as an adventure playground – where are the edible weeds

One Huffington Post pundit predicts rewilding to be the next big human movement, a kind of post-environmentalism.

and food trees? Where are the fox dens? Where are the birds nesting? I like to ask people 'tourist test' questions to see how much they know about their bioregion. Questions like 'Which way does the wet weather usually come in from?', 'Where is the moon in its cycle right now?', 'What is the nearest wild edible at your backdoor?' and 'Where does your water come from when it comes out of the tap? And then where does it go?'. Often people are quite shocked to realise how much they don't know or take for granted.

Urban rewilding is also about 'switching' on the senses again, as if you needed them to survive. It's about remembering the invisible systems that support our existence – water, food, fire, air. How much of a direct relationship can I have with my food? How much can I grow in my small backyard? Can I trace where all my food comes from, visit the farms and befriend the growers? What are the interactions between the wild and the domestic food sources? Exploring local foraging, community gardens, urban forestry and guerrilla gardening. It's about countering the sedentary nature of city life and using our bodies in a variety of ways.

Urban rewilding has much in common with the slow travel movement. Can you share a couple of your own slow travel moments?
Slowing down is a key concept for urban rewilding. We miss so much in our city haste. It's so easy to get stuck in the rut of routine and to be ruled by the to-do list. Sometimes I catch myself rushing to get to the end of my tasks so then real life can start. In reality, the demands on us are like a magic pudding – there is always something else calling for our attention. My sit spot, the call of the first bird of the morning, the twilight dusk, the first yellow-tailed black cockatoo arriving in my backyard in autumn – none of these announce their presence with a 'ping'. It takes a certain awareness and discipline to step away from the fast pace of life and attend to these quieter voices, these slower cycles. Curiosity is a fantastic quality to cultivate in order to slow down and take notice. If like me you're curious about the seasonal change indicators then you will step outside first thing in the morning and listen. You will take notice of where the weather is coming from, what the insects are doing, the bees.

Travelling is a great opportunity to experience the quality of wandering without time or destination. I remember setting off in the back alleys of Venice with no map and time constraints. I could follow whim, curiosity and intuition, which led me to some strange and wonderful rabbit burrows.

How can travellers urban rewild? Any tips?
Without our routine ruts of awareness, being a foreigner in a foreign country is an opportune time to experience expanded sensory awareness. Greet the new place as if you're a curious creature – what does it smell like, taste like? What are the quietest sounds in the distance and the most prominent? What time is dawn and dusk? What is the bodily 'felt sense' of this place? Ditch the GPS and set out on a day-long wander without time or destination, following your nose, or your 'navel-gation,' open to adventure and surprise. Seek out the green spaces and forage for some of the wild edibles like plantain and dandelion and mallow that are found the world over. Find out where the water that you drink is coming from – connect the city to the overall catchment. Take off your shoes in a park and let the earth of this place rise up to greet you.

> **Without our routine ruts of awareness, being a foreigner in a foreign country is an opportune time to experience expanded sensory awareness.**

UNION GLACIER
ANTARCTICA
79°46'S 82°52'W
9613 SM LONDON
10352 SM MOSCOW
PUNTA ARENAS 2991 KM
9464 SM PARIS
14500 KM
LOS ANGELES 12850 KM
10296 SM OSLO
8531 SM TORONTO
TOKYO 14770 KM
SYDNEY 6949 KM
11732 SM NORTH POLE
SOUTH POLE 1138 KM
9843 SM

CONCLUSION

Rewilding and urban rewilding are intricately linked with the slow travel movement. For working urbanised people with busy lives (and that's most of us), slow travel offers one of the few windows where time and the natural world synchronise. I hope, in the pages of this book, be it through the words or the pictures, you have been inspired to find your own place of solace and sense of self in nature and travel. Perhaps it was in the Animal instinct chapter, befriending other citizen scientists in mountainous Transylvania on a quest to monitor the bears, wolves, lynx and bison. Or in South Africa joining the Ulwazi Research Programme to see the progress of rewilded aardvarks, honey badgers and leopards. The Cultural immersion chapter may have motivated you to learn how to survive solo on mountain treks or, in the Go beyond chapter, fend for yourself in the Borneo jungle.

But slow travel and rewilding don't have to be extreme. Like forest bathing, there are gradients of accomplishment and I've wanted to cater for them. In the Boltholes chapter, Glen Dye Cabins offering hipster comfort in the wild might have caught your attention, or perhaps the off-grid Beach Hut in South Devon has helped you map out a way to put your toes within reach of the waves and not much else.

In fact, many of the slow journeys mentioned in this book are rewilding opportunities, where taking the time to connect on a deeper level with yourself, the destination and the world you are passing through is at the heart of it all. Whether you're on foot, bike, boat or train in remote and wild locations or in built-up cities finding your inner light in the night, the aim is to slow right down and take the time to truly connect with the world around you. Wherever your adventures take you, may your travels be slow.

Left: Union Glacier Camp, Antarctica, is, happily, a long way from everywhere

INDEX

ABOUT THE AUTHOR

Award-winning writer, journalist and author Penny Watson has travelled the world, written feature articles for countless magazines and newspapers, and researched a number of guidebooks including *Hong Kong Precincts* and *London Pocket Precincts*. As her career has evolved so has Penny's yearning for slow travel. This book, and one of her upcoming titles, *Ultimate Campsites: Australia*, are a direct response to this need. She is a member of both the British Guild of Travel Writers, and Australian Society of Travel Writers. She currently resides in Melbourne with her partner Pippy and their two children Digby and Etienne.

ACKNOWLEDGEMENTS

Big thanks to the Hardie Grant team for publishing my third solo book. And especially to editors Megan Cuthbert and Alexander Payne for pulling it all together, and publisher Melissa Kayser, who first sent me that tantalising email seeding the idea of a slow travel book. *Slow Travel* was largely written in Melbourne coffee shops and at my dining table. But the inspiration came from two decades of incredibly inspiring and life-changing travel, both personal and professional. Thanks always to my partner Pipster whose adventurous spirit, grounded nature and ever-present support has enabled much of it to happen. During the school holidays, I turned my (small) walk-in robe into a make-shift office – thanks to my loving and beautiful children Digby and Etienne who put up with my part-time mothering while I got the job done.

PHOTO CREDITS

Published in 2019 by Hardie Grant Travel,
a division of Hardie Grant Publishing

Hardie Grant Travel (Melbourne)
Building 1, 658 Church Street
Richmond, Victoria 3121

Hardie Grant Travel (Sydney)
Level 7, 45 Jones Street
Ultimo, NSW 2007

www.hardiegrant.com/au/travel

**A catalogue record for this
book is available from the
National Library of Australia**

Slow Travel
ISBN 9781741176674

10 9 8 7 6 5 4 3 2 1

Publisher
Melissa Kayser
Senior editor
Megan Cuthbert
Project Editor
Alexandra Payne
Editorial assistance
Rosanna Dutson
Proofreader
Tanya Eccleston
Design
Kåre Martens, madebyhandverk.no
Typesetting
Kerry Cooke
Index
Max McMaster
Prepress
Kerry Cooke and Splitting Image Colour Studio

Printed and bound in China by LEO Paper Products LTD.